Avery,

You Are Awesome!

Enjoy THE Book!

57 Outs

&

11 Hours in Baseball Purgatory

WILLIAM B MOSLEY

Table of Contents

Acknowledgments

To my family:
My parents Bill and Beatrice Mosley, thank you for allowing me to chase my dreams. My brother, Tarence, for always being my number one fan, and my sister, Erin, for dealing with an overachieving brother.

To those that supported my youth sports:
Gary Passama, Chuck Hammond, Jerone Williams and Marvin Clark...
Thank you for investing in me.

To my coaches:
Juan Medina, Brad Hanson, Rob Bruno, Kevin Ratterman, Tim Jamison, Jim Barr, Norm Thompson and Todd Smith...
Thank you for teaching me how to play baseball and become a man.

To the families that supported my youth coaching:
Chamaine and Paul Elder, Eugene and Marci Escalante, Byron Berhel, Rick and Ginger Alspaw, Ed Gibbons, Jenelle and Todd Delorfice, Lea and Lance Uyeno, Isolde and Alec Wilson, Ananda and Jason Tavano, Kimberly and Walt Schmidt, Desire and Alfred Robles, Jim Pitcher, and Beatrice and Marcel Etchevery...
Thank you for all of your financial and moral support.

To the Drake community:
Nate Severin, Chad Stuart, Anne Capron, Scott Lance, Gary Roth and Tom Brown...
Thank you for trusting and believing in me.

To my literary contributors:
Adam Farb, Keegan Pedersen, Danny Schmidt, Elon Lewis-Wallace, Karima Wallace, and Nancy Moore...
Thank you for making this book a reality.

Foreword

In a seemingly odd response to my account of some version of the story in these pages, I remember my grandmother telling me about a funeral and a pastor she once knew long ago, eulogizing to his grieving congregation in a small church in suburban Georgia. Sweltering in that uniquely muggy Georgian air, she listened from the pew as the pastor talked about stories and why they matter. He told her that one of the most important things we can do in this world is tell stories.

Stories are heirlooms we pass down. They are the memories of life and the people we love and the treasures we all leave behind, more valuable than precious diamonds or solid gold. As that pastor knew, stories bring comfort, joy, a respite along the journey. If stories cease to be told, their memory will disappear in time.

This is our story. It is about baseball and circumstance, failure and redemption, and the tinge of mystery and magic that accompany many great feats. It is about the very large and sometimes unjust obstacles that lie in the base paths of everyday life. It is about the very small, like the blades of grass that guide a worn ball into a perfect 6-4-3 double play under midnight lights. And, it is about more than baseball, about finding a million ways to lose, and winning.

In some ways, this story is our own eulogy, of the games and moments in between that are now gone, and of friends and adversaries that will be too. More than anything, it is a celebration of joy exploding from thin air, of countless things that weren't supposed to happen, that couldn't possibly happen, but did.

To a game that felt like it would last forever, and hopefully will. Enjoy our crazy marathon game and fantastic season through my coach's eyes…

~Keegan Pedersen, Drake Baseball Class of 2017

Introduction

The idea for this book came about after a phone interview with a writer from the *San Francisco Chronicle* following the 2017 season. I was describing our accomplishments to him and he joked that it sounded like fiction. It took a few weeks, but after the championship glow began to wear off, I thought about what the writer said and realized we did have a pretty good story to tell.

When I took over as the varsity coach a few years ago, I developed the Core 4 Focus and began to weave it into everything that we did. The 2017 team was, by far, the most focused team I have ever coached.

Core 4 Focus is very simple. I evaluate my players using just four things: Attention, Attitude, Effort, and Endurance.

Attention
- Do they know the outs?
- Do they know the score?
- Do they know where the next play is?
- Do they know who is good on the other team?

Attitude
- How do they act when they struggle/succeed?
- How do they treat teammates when they struggle/succeed?
- Do they hold on to the past too long?
- Do they bring off-field struggles on to the field?

Effort
- How hard do they practice?
- How hard do they condition?
- Do they have to be told to hustle?
- Does their effort change based on results?

Endurance
- How do they finish drills?
- How do they finish practices?
- How do they finish games?
- How do they finish seasons?

Core 4 Focus has nothing to do with size, speed, or talent. It is about creating the right mentality for success in a game that is filled with failure. The players totally bought in and were able to accomplish something incredible.

The 2017 team didn't have any four-year college prospects and only two players from the team went on to play in junior college. We were not overpowering offensively, and our pitchers didn't light up the radar gun, but we never beat ourselves. We never gave up the big inning. We didn't allow a team to score more than three runs in any of our thirty games. As a matter of fact, we played 221 innings and only gave up more than a single run in four of them.

This is a story about a special team, one amazing game, and the longest, strangest night of my coaching life. My mind took me on a wild ride down memory lane, bringing back some of my ghosts of seasons past while replaying every mistake and bad decision from eighteen innings of fantastic baseball. The minutes felt like hours and I was held captive by my thoughts from 1:00am Friday night until 12:00pm on Saturday.

Thankfully, we won the game and finished off a sensational season. Happy endings and 19th inning walk-off homeruns are wonderful, but behind every heroic moment is a struggle to get there. This book details my eleven hours in baseball purgatory between the 18th and 19th innings of the Drake vs. Marin Catholic, Marin County Athletic League Championship game, on Friday, May 19 and Saturday May 20, 2017, a scorebook breakdown, random thoughts from my baseball mind, and the magical experiences that followed.

2017 MCAL and NCS Division III Champion Drake Pirates

Chapter 1 – Attention

Attention: *the action of dealing with or taking special care of someone or something*
Paying Attention is *the notice taken of someone or something; the regarding of someone or something as interesting or important*

- Physical: Keep your eyes and ears open.
- Mental: Identify and process information from situations, surroundings, and body language.
- Self-Check: Why am I here?

1:00am

Jackie had had an accident. I could smell it as I opened the door to my upstairs one-bedroom apartment. I couldn't expect a four-month-old puppy to hold himself together for seven hours. He had been expecting me three hours earlier. Named after my hero Jackie Robinson, he was always happy to see me. He was an Italian Greyhound and Chihuahua mix with long legs and an adorable face.

Jackie Robinson's first day on the field

Jackie helping with the bats

He'd only been in my life for two months, but he'd already become my best friend and the team mascot. He didn't care how many times I screwed up tonight. He was always happy to see me win, lose, or tie, but tonight was going to be a long one. I squandered so many opportunities to put the game away. I blew it. I didn't step up and lead my players when they needed me most.

High school baseball games typically last about two hours, but we'd just played for five and a half and we still didn't have a winner. Eighteen innings of baseball and we were still tied. We had so many chances to win and so many emotional ups and downs.

The crowd would swell up, just to be disappointed over and over again. Now all we could do was wait.

Sellout Crowd at Albert Park

The City of San Rafael shut us down because of a midnight city curfew. The MCAL Championship game had been played at Albert Park for as long as I could remember. Constructed in 1940, the stadium was a charming throwback to the days of small "band box" ballparks where the game was played close to the fans. It is the current home of the San Rafael Pacific's independent professional baseball team.

There was no way that I was going to get any sleep. I had eleven hours until we had to be on the field to finish a game that might never end. I'd never been a part of anything quite like this.

In baseball, it is very beneficial to have a short memory and a lot of patience. This game had been a part of my daily life since I was four years old, yet thirty-six years later, I was still seeing some things for the first time. I struggled to wrap my head around what had just happened. How many times could we give away the game?? We had countless opportunities to put it away with one good at-bat. We had the bases loaded time and time again. I didn't call a single squeeze play, just strikeouts, double plays, and bone-headed base coaching. The score was 1-1 and we had struck out eighteen times and left nineteen runners on base. That was practically unbelievable. I wouldn't have believed it, if I, along with 2,000 people, hadn't seen it with our own eyes.

How I Ended Up at Drake

Sir Francis Drake High School is nestled between San Rafael, Fairfax, and Ross in the town of San Anselmo, with a population of roughly 12,000 residents and a downtown that features statues of Yoda and Indiana Jones. My first interaction with the school came in 1995 as a senior at Vanden High School in Fairfield. Our basketball team lost in overtime against the Pirates in the Nor Cal Semifinals. I scored 27 points but went 4-10 from the free-throw line in fourth quarter and overtime. It wasn't until I started coaching at Drake fifteen years later that I realized that it wasn't a private school.

I first met Adam Farb in Las Vegas in July of 2009. He was hosting a 13U World Series tournament and I had brought a team from Fairfield. I had a player on my team that was as hot as the 120-degree weather.

He won the Offensive Player of the Tournament award, even though our team was eliminated early. The turf was so hot that I lost two pairs of shoes during that tournament. The soles literally melted apart on the field. It was so hot that the tournament table literally burst into flames. Adam had been giving out a crystal trophy to the champion and combination of direct sunlight and wind created the perfect spark. Sometimes things just come together at the right time and something special happens. Adam had just completed his first season as the varsity baseball coach at Drake HS and he needed a JV coach for the upcoming season. I had applied for the Fairfield HS varsity position and was passed over.

Working with Adam opened my eyes to the business aspect of travel baseball and introduced me to USA baseball. My first experience was at the USA Baseball National Team Identification Series in Cary, North Carolina in August of 2010. I coached a very talented 13U team with Nate Trosky that represented the Northern California region. We played in a four-game round robin tournament with eleven other regions from around the country with more than 190 players, all hoping to be one of the lucky few players to be chosen to represent their country. Our roster was filled with NCAA Division I talent. We had seven players selected to attend the USA National team trials. It was a great experience for me to be around that caliber of baseball as a coach.

2010 Northern California 13U NTIS Roster Highlights:

- *Thirteen players received Division I baseball scholarships from the following schools: Arizona State, Stanford (3 players), UC Davis, Oregon State (3 players), University of Pacific, St. Mary's College, UC Berkeley and Sacramento State (2 players)*
- *One player was drafted by and signed with the Oakland A's in 2015*
- *One player was Pac 12 player of the year in 2017*
- *One player was West Coast Conference Freshman of the year in 2017*
- *4th overall pick in 2018 draft*
- *20th overall pick in 2018 draft*
- *24th overall pick in 2018 draft*

I began to broaden my horizons as a strategist as well. My first year at Drake, we were forced to use wood bats because of a tragic line drive accident with a varsity pitcher the season before.

I had to learn how to manufacture runs and develop a pitching staff. Adam took me to the Ultimate Pitching Coaches Boot Camp at the Texas Baseball Ranch in Montgomery, Texas in December 2011. That was where I met the Wolforths. Ron and Jill Wolforth are the first family when it comes to developing pitchers.

Although the first time we officially met was on their ranch in Texas, it wasn't the first time they noticed me. Their son played with the Texas region at the USA NTIS event and saw me working with the Northern California team. I wasn't hard to miss, being the only African-American coach at the event.

Jill told me she liked the way I worked with players and wanted to know if her son could join my team for the USA National Championship in Arizona in the summer of 2012. He could have gone with any of the power programs in Texas, but I was flattered that his parents wanted him with me. I like to think that anyway. They just wanted him to play with good players. Our roster was loaded with players from Northern California, Oklahoma, and Texas.

2012 15U USA National Championships Roster Highlights:

- *8 players received Division I baseball scholarships from the following schools: Loyola Marymount, Boston College, UC Santa Barbara, University of Utah, UC Davis, Dallas Baptist, Texas A&M, and the University of Iowa*
- *One player was drafted by and signed with the Cleveland Indians in 2017*

Along with coaching high-level talent, I also attended my first American Baseball Coaches Association National Convention in January 2012. It was the first time I took my professional development seriously, and thanks to Adam, I haven't missed an ABCA convention since.

Sir Francis Drake/Marin Catholic Rivalry

Once I started coaching at Drake, it didn't take me long to realize that the only private school located on Sir Francis Drake Boulevard is Marin Catholic. I also quickly learned that despite Drake and Marin Catholic sharing the same street, they are a million miles apart philosophically. There is a deep-seeded disdain between the schools that goes back more than thirty years. For many years, the barometer for a successful Drake sports team was how they did against MC. This year, we swept them in the regular season. For the seniors, it was the first time they had ever beaten them. My last two years as JV coach, I only lost four total MCAL games, all to MC. Unfortunately, that streak carried over to my first year as varsity coach, with one of the losses being on a walk-off homerun at their place last year.

To say that tonight's game had extra meaning was an understatement. No Drake baseball team had ever beaten MC three times in a season, and the players were well aware of the history. We also were aware that they were peaking at the right time. We limped into the MCAL playoffs after clinching the #1 seed early and then "mailing in" the last two regular season games with lackluster baseball, resulting in back-to-back losses. MC had won the MCAL tournament last year, and we knew that we'd have to bring it to win both banners. As the fans starting filing in and the sun began to set, the battle was just beginning.

Pitching At A Premium

Going into last year's offseason, my most pressing concern was pitching depth. I had no idea who my #2 through #5 pitchers would be. We had eighteen league games and we played two games a week, except for two three-game weeks.

With the new pitch count and rest rules, I had to be very strategic with my rotation. In a perfect world, I would always want my ace to pitch in every big game, but I don't coach in that world. I used five pitchers in the regular season.

1. Nick Roth - 81 innings with 13 appearances
2. Ryan McLaughlin - 77.2 innings with 14 appearances
3. Owen Hamilton - 31.2 innings with 10 appearances
4. Keegan Pedersen - 14.2 innings with 7 appearances
5. Spencer Graves - 16 innings with 5 appearances

Lowest team ERA in the country

We used our #1 starter, senior, Nick Roth, in the semifinal game against San Marin, so our #2 junior, Ryan McLaughlin, got the start tonight. He pitched very well all season but never had to face the top tier teams. I'm pretty sure that he had never pitched in front of a packed house in a championship game before. Ryan had a 6-1 record with a microscopic 0.37 ERA during the regular season.

Number two starter Ryan McLaughlin

Ryan stepped up and separated himself from the herd. He came into high school a meek and mild 5'10" 165-pound skinny kid. He had grown and worked himself into a 6'2" 195-pound stud. By his third start of the year, he was the clear #2. Even with four shutouts under his belt coming into tonight, he still felt like he had something to prove on the big stage.

Game On

The excitement at the game tonight was palatable. The energy in the crowd was electric and school spirit was in full force. Drake fans on the third base side were wearing green, and the MC fans on the first base side were wearing navy blue. The bleachers were packed, and we could feel the weight of the game beginning to build as the first pitch was thrown.

C.J. Castillo stepped to the plate as the leadoff batter for MC to the sounds of "HE'S A TRAITOR" yelled in unison from the Drake fans. He had been a member of the Pirates 2015 NCS Championship team as one of two freshmen on the varsity team. He transferred to MC his sophomore year and the student section was letting him have it for going to the dark side. Loud and a bit obnoxious, the crowd was ready to go.

1st Inning

<u>Top</u>
Castillo – Strikeout
Petersen – Pop out to 2nd base
Armusewicz – Fly out to right field
<u>Bottom</u>
Leary – Fly out to center field
Delst – Pop out to 3rd base
Roth – Single, stolen base
Lance – Fly out to center field

2nd Inning

<u>Top</u>
Bentley – Reached on error, run scored
Joyce – Base on balls
Caravello – Sacrifice bunt to pitcher
Mauterer – Sacrifice fly, RBI
Skinner – Fly out to right field
<u>Bottom</u>
Hamilton – Fly out to right field
McLaughlin – Strikeout
Clark – Strikeout

Early Game Jitters

We were the first team to crack. Owen made a nervous error at first base in the 2nd inning. He fielded a ground ball and made an alligator arm throw directly to the pitcher's feet in the top of the 2nd. That runner ended up scoring on a sacrifice fly and, just like that, we were down 1-0.

Owen wanted to beat MC more than any other player. I could see in his eyes just how badly he wanted to win as he walked back to the dugout. Going back to his first two years of high school as a JV player, he was on the mound as a freshman and sophomore with a chance to win the JV title and lost both times in heartbreaking fashion.

After we gave up the first run, I looked around our bench and there was not one shred of doubt. It was the same feeling I had had on the first day with this group. They possessed a focused confidence that made them very fun to coach. Our team was senior-heavy with a strong group of underclassmen as well.

So when Owen got back to the dugout after the 2nd-inning error, he had nineteen guys and five coaches picking him up. We also knew that was probably all they were going to get. Even down 1-0, this group had real confidence in themselves and the ability of their teammates.

Our Experienced Leaders

The starting lineup featured three seniors, three juniors, and three sophomores. I'd coached most of the team for at least three years because I was with them at the JV level too. For Jensen, Owen, Nick, and Patrick, it had been all four. That type of relationship was rare in high school. I could read their body language and they could read mine. They had become an extension of me on the field.

Jensen was my defensive leader. He called all the plays and directed traffic. Despite being only 5'2" and 120 pounds, he had played like a giant all four years. He made up for his size with speed and intelligence and was also an All-League wide receiver and valedictorian with a 4.5 GPA. He was the starting shortstop on my JV team as a freshman and sophomore. He played second base last year, but this year, he went back to his home at shortstop and we benefited greatly from his leadership.

Jensen Yamane working Pre-Game

Jensen getting into tag position

We hadn't given up more than three runs in a single game.

Furthermore, we had only given up more than one run at a time in two innings all season. Jensen knew how to find the hidden outs. He excelled at calling for back picks, pickoffs, bunt defensive execution, and 1st & 3rd defenses at the right time. He understood my expectations and relayed that to the infield without being told. He even coached travel baseball in his spare time. There are many times when I asked him what he thought and ended up going with whatever he said.

Owen was probably the only person that loved baseball more than I did. He always had a big smile on his face but was a lot tougher than he looked. He enjoyed the grind of baseball. The work was fun to him. He also played water polo, never missed morning weights, and, was the salutatorian with a 4.5 GPA. He forced his way onto the JV team as a 5'8", 140-pound freshman. Even after he wasn't offered a spot on the team, he continued to come to practice anyway. By the end of the season, he was in the starting lineup.

He was the unanimous team MVP his sophomore year. He won the Golden Arm and Silver Slugger awards as well. He threw two no-hitters and three one-hitters without breaking 73 mph. He also hit .450. His junior year, Owen was injured and couldn't pitch, but he played first base and had a good offensive year. He batted .380 with twenty-two singles and only one RBI. At the suggestion of one of his teammates, he turned himself into a sidearm pitcher this year. Although he still didn't throw very hard, he knew how to keep the ball down and get outs. He had only given up one earned run in twenty-four innings this season. Now at six feet, 175 pounds, his bat had been good for us and he continued to show signs of power with two home runs.

Owen Hamilton dropping down

Nick was our "horse." He came into high school a pudgy 5'7", 160-pound kid. He had transformed into a good athlete and now at 5'10", 190 pounds, he had earned the respect of all his teammates. He could be fiery at times but might play better when he was mad. He was our emotional leader. I brought him up to the JV team midway through his freshman year. He became one of our best players right away. His ability to hit the ball the other way and stay back on off-speed pitches allowed him to get called up to varsity as a sophomore in 2015. Nick went 4-3 with a 1.01 ERA and batted .343 with 15 RBI last year. This year, he was at it again, with a record 7-3 with ten complete games on mound and batting .348 in the third spot in the order.

Number one starter Nick Roth

Patrick was a jack-of-all-trades. He had done a little bit of everything during his four years with me. He started out pitching for me on the JV team as a freshman and had literally played every other position since then. He played third when Nick pitched and tonight I think I had him in right field. He was a model teammate and well-respected by his peers. He also played soccer and basketball and was an outstanding student with a 4.4 GPA.

I was rooting for these guys. I wanted them to go out with a bang because I had seen all the work they had put in. They dedicated themselves to getting better. From the weight room to off-season training, my seniors had set the tone for the entire program without saying a word.

I was witness to their struggles and was impressed by the way they embraced their failures. They used each as motivation to improve and eventually succeed. So far this season, they had done everything I had asked them to do and brought the younger guys right along with them.

3rd Inning

<u>Top</u>
Harris – Fly out to right field
Castillo – Ground out to pitcher
Petersen – Pop out to 3rd base
<u>Bottom</u>
Brockley – Strikeout
Yamane – Fly out to center field
Leary – Fly out to right field

MC definitely had our *attention*. Trailing after three innings, we were in a ball game. This was exactly what we wanted and worked hard for all season long. It felt like a game that was going to come down to the end, and so far, this season, the boys had been up for every challenge.

MCAL Regular Season Champions

The Marin County Athletic League has ten varsity baseball teams. Drake, Marin Catholic, Redwood, Tamalpais, San Rafael, Terra Linda, San Marin, Novato, Branson, and Justin-Siena. In 2015, four teams won NCS titles, which is unheard of for one league. In other words, the MCAL Championship can sometimes be tougher than section playoffs. Everyone played twice, which makes for a grueling eighteen-game league schedule. We finished in first place with a record of 14-4, but the crown jewel of the MCAL was the post-season tournament championship.

Even before tonight, they had already had a successful season. It was the best season start in school history at 12-0, regular season MCAL champions and a high seed in the NCS Division III playoffs next week, but they came into tonight wanting more.

The top six teams qualify with the top two teams receiving a first-round bye. We beat San Marin 6-1 on Wednesday night with the help of a grand slam from Ryan, and a solid pitching performance from Nick. MC beat Redwood 2-0 on Thursday night, setting up a showdown between the top two regular season teams.

Gallery A

Drake baseball wins season opener

By Marin Independent Journal

POSTED: 03/02/17, 9:23 PM PST | UPDATED: ON
03/02/2017

Rocky Clark went 3 for 3 with a run scored, helping the Drake High baseball team beat Moreau Catholic 2-1 in its season opener on Wednesday.

Nick Roth was solid on the mound, tossing six innings of four- hit ball with seven strikeouts, two walks and one earned run surrendered. Keegan Pedersen notched the save for the Pirates.

Boys Prep of the Week: Case Delst

POSTED: 03/13/17, 6:39 PM PDT | UPDATED: ON
03/13/2017

What he did: In two victories last week, the junior went a combined 2 for 5 with a run scored and five RBIs for the unbeaten Pirates. He sent a first-pitch fastball over the left-center wall for a grand slam against Windsor, raising his batting average to .400. Delst is the team's lone remaining starter from the section-title-winning squad in 2015.

What he said: "I didn't really think about hitting a grand slam, I just wanted to put a good swing on it and come through for my team. Obviously I'm happy with the result. It's something that we haven't really had a lot at Drake before, so starting off this well is a big confidence booster for us. We're doing everything we need to do to be a successful team right now."

What's next: The undefeated Pirates (5-0) open league play at
Marin Catholic on Tuesday.

— Danny Schmidt

"He's my most experienced player, even though he's just a junior. This year he's worked really, really hard to be a leader, and he's off to a great start offensively."

Will Mosley: Drake coach on Delst's performance thus far this season.

Marin baseball: Team-by-team preview capsules

By Danny Schmidt, *Marin Independent Journal*

POSTED: 03/13/17, 6:17 PM PDT | UPDATED: ON
03/14/2017

With consistent rain throughout the preseason, Marin County high school baseball teams got creative.

Players have spent the past month fielding ground balls on turf football fields, sprinting around basketball gyms, playing catch on tennis courts and in school hallways, and spending ample time hitting inside cages. By the time league play begins Tues- day, most teams will have had less than five practices on their own field.

"We're probably the best Whiffle ball team in the league," Marin Academy coach Ron Robinson said.

Because of the weather, pitchers will most likely be ahead of the curve, which is typically the case with MCAL teams, regardless of weather. The usual suspects are expected to be strong once again, led by Redwood and Marin Catholic, the respective reigning regular-season and tournament champions.

Drake and Tam are full of key returners, and Branson and San Marin are likely to find themselves in the postseason hunt. A handful of coaches have predicted a solid season from San Rafael, which looks to end its MCAL playoff drought that extends back to its new coach's playing days over a decade ago.

"Everybody's got returning guys and some young talent, as well," Terra Linda coach Patrick Conroy said. "I think it will be similar to last year, where all but one team was fighting for that last playoff spot until the last day of the year."

Similar to last season, with a shortened preseason that featured limited non-league action, coaches will rely heavily on depth, specifically on the mound.

"You have to be ready," San Marin coach Jamie Vattuone said, "because, ready or not, MCAL starts on Tuesday."

DRAKE

Coach: Will Mosley (second season) Current record: 5-0
Last season: 15-12, 11-7 (tied for third in MCAL); lost in quarter finals of NCS D-III playoffs

NCS classification: Division III

Outlook: Mosley, who felt the Pirates underachieved last season, said the team has a new, stronger mindset this spring. Drake returns plenty of talent, including ace Nick Roth, who batted .343 and boasted a 1.01 ERA last season en route to earning second-team all-league honors. Owen Hamilton (.375 batting average), Jensen Yamane (.343) and Case Delst (.261) all return after exceptional seasons in 2016. Mosley is starting three sophomores — Gabe Leary, Eamonn Lance and Isaac Friedenberg — and senior first baseman Rocky Clark has emerged as a standout. Junior Ryan McLaughlin will assist Roth and Keegan Pedersen on the bump.

The last word: "I think this year there is a different tone set by our leaders," Mosley said. "The goal for our team this year is to win both banners from the MCAL. There's a collective joy sur- rounding this team. All seventeen players want to be there every day and we're enjoying the grind together."

MARIN CATHOLIC

Coach: Jesse Foppert (fifth season)

Current record: 0-3

Last season: 23-5, 15-3 (second in MCAL); won league tournament, lost in quarterfinals of NCS D-II playoffs

NCS classification: Division II

Outlook: The Wildcats return a handful of key pieces from last season's team, which won the MCAL tournament at Albert Park. A trio of standout seniors lead the way for Marin Catholic: Casey Armusewicz batted .337 and drove in thirteen runs en route to earning first-team all-league honors last season; Joe Levin is one of the top catchers in the county; and Hayden Wellbeloved finished last spring 3-0 with a 0.66 ERA in 21 1/3 innings pitched. Joining Wellbeloved on the pitching staff — one of the best in the MCAL — this season are Addison Berger, Jack Harris, and a few others. Marin Catholic graduated a stellar pair of aces in Brandon Buckley and Mike Praszker, who both now play for Santa Clara.

The last word: "I like where we're headed," Foppert said. "We definitely need to get better, but that's everybody. There's always things to work on, and for us to reach our goals this year, we need to continue to get better every day. I think we'll definitely be able to lean (our experience) at times. All those kids who were brought up from JV or the bench players from last season are now going to have a bigger role. It was great for them to be a part of it."

Drake uncorks on San Marin, improves to 7-0

By Danny Schmidt, *Marin Independent Journal*

POSTED: 03/17/17, 8:40 PM PDT | UPDATED: ON 03/18/2017

As Owen Hamilton glided around the bases following a second-inning grand slam, it became apparent just how dangerous the Drake High baseball team is this season.

Hamilton's blast gave the Pirates a 9-0 lead and sealed what would become a 12-1 victory against San Marin in a matchup of premier area teams on Friday in San Anselmo.

"They're rolling, they're playing great baseball, and they're the team to beat," San Marin coach Jamie

Vattuone said.

Hamilton led the undefeated Pirates (7-0, 2-0 MCAL), going 2 for 3 with a walk, two runs scored and five RBIs, as well as pitching two scoreless innings in relief. In its seven victories this season, Drake has outscored opponents a combined 48-7.

"We didn't expect to have an ERA under 1.00 after seven games," Drake coach Will Mosley said. "The way we're playing right now is really, really fun. Guys are just stepping up and the moment isn't getting too big. Everything that's happening right now is from hard work."

Two San Marin errors in the bottom of the first inning allowed Drake to jump out to a 3-0 lead, despite Case Delst (2 for 2, two runs) recording the only hit in the frame. A pair of hit batsmen and a walk to begin the bottom of the second loaded the bases with no outs for Nick Roth, who reached on an RBI infield single.

Hamilton watched his way to a 2-0 count, then drove a fastball over the left-field wall for a grand slam, putting the game out of reach before the Mustangs recorded a fourth out.

"I was ahead in the count, so I knew I could take a rip," Hamilton said. "I thought it was going to go off the wall, but it went right over the top. It was a great feeling.

"We were trying to add on. Even when we had nine runs, we were trying to add on because you never know what's going to happen in a baseball game. That did give us a cushion."

The 9-0 lead remained intact until the top of the fifth inning, when pinch-hitter Dalton Eckert got the Mustangs on the board by plating Matt Lozovoy with a single up the middle.

Drake's Matt Brockley entered Friday's contest with one hit on the season: a bunt. The senior led off the bottom of the fifth as a pinch-hitter, and he delivered on a much more full swing than his first tally, sending a rocket over the left-field wall for a solo homer to give Drake a 10-1 advantage.

The Pirates added two unearned runs in the sixth. Isaac Friedenberg and Eric Woodrow each scored, the latter coming in on a two-out double from Hamilton, who raised his season average to .381.

Ryan McLaughlin was solid on the mound for Drake, striking out six over five innings. Starter Jason Franks (four innings) and Beau Thompson combined on the Mustangs' pitching effort, striking out a total of seven batters. The lopsided score allowed the teams to send a combined thirty-one players to the plate.

"They played great, jumped on our mistakes, and buried us," Vattuone said. "We have to learn from it. What we said is the baseball gods got us, because we were all high and mighty after a big win against Redwood (on Tuesday), and we came and laid an egg today.

"Every game in MCAL is going to be tough, and we just didn't show up today. I would like to think we're a better team than that. We'll see. Luckily, we have sixteen more."

San Marin faces cross-town rival Novato on Tuesday, while Drake looks for a bit of revenge against Tam in Mill Valley.

"It's going to be huge," Mosley said. "They knocked us out of the MCAL tournament last year with a (game-ending) triple play, so all these guys are ready to play. We like having games we get up for, so we won't have any problem getting excited."

Chapter 2 – Attitude

Attitude: *a settled way of thinking or feeling about someone or something, typically one that is reflected in a person's behavior*

- Physical: Walk, run and speak with confidence.

- Mental: Success is never permanent, and failure is never fatal.

- Self-Check: What does my reflection look like?

4:00am:

I just got a text from another one of my players telling me he couldn't sleep. I felt his pain. I tried a few times, but I just tossed and turned in my bed. I even tried watching Netflix and playing a game on my PS4, but just couldn't shut off the game in my head. I'd had plenty of sleepless nights as a coach, but tonight was something different altogether. Normally, I would stew over a loss, going over everything that I did wrong and replaying the game in a loop in my mind all night. By the morning, I could usually move on, unless it was the final game of the season.

My *attitude* comes directly from my dealings with failure and my coaching career had provided plenty of chances for growth.

A History of Mistakes

In 2013, I made a coaching blunder that eliminated my 15U team from the Team USA national championship tournament.

I used an ineligible player to courtesy run, and, when we tied the game up, that runner was called out and there was nothing I could do about it. I screwed up the rule, and, just like that, our tournament had been over. I locked myself in my hotel room for the rest of the trip. I passed up an expensive free dinner with some of the best baseball minds. It was one of the worst feelings in the world because I felt personally responsible for ending the tournament for fifteen players.

Coaches rarely lose sleep when they win. My 2016 team kept me up quite a bit. We lost six games with the lead in the bottom of the 7th. Four of the games, we still had the lead with two outs. Those were the types of losses that lead to ulcers and hair loss for coaches. Sometimes I couldn't sleep the night before a big game. Butterflies and "what ifs" kept me awake with the anticipation of the upcoming competition. Tonight was a combination of both. I realized that we were a part of something special, but the suspense was killing me.

In 2016, we ended with a 15-12 overall record but easily could have been 21-6 if we didn't fall apart during the final three outs of those games. We finished the regular season as the #4 seed and lost to #5 Tamalpais in heartbreaking fashion, even though we never had the lead.

The Triple Play Game 2016

We were trailing 4-3 in the bottom of the 7th. We managed to get runners on first and second with 0 outs. Tam put in a freshman left-handed pitcher that was obviously nervous. Before the pitching change, I put a pinch hitter on deck for one of my senior outfielders, who was disappointed with my decision. After the pitching change, I put the original hitter back on deck because it was a bunt situation and he was one of our best bunters. Still visibly shaken from my coaching moves, he responded with poor body language when I gave the sign for a sacrifice bunt. Not only would he have moved the tying run to third and the winning run to second with only one out, but my belief was that the freshman might throw the ball down the right field line.

After two unsuccessful attempts, the count was 0-2. On the third pitch, he put a soft liner in play toward centerfield. For a moment, it looked like it was going to drop in for a single, so the runner from second took off looking to score and the runner from first was nearly halfway when the centerfielder came in and made a running shin-high catch. There was stunned silence on both sides of the field. Even the umpires had to pause for a moment to realize what was happening as they threw the ball to second and then on to first. Triple play. Game over.

We did manage to win an NCS game and the player that hit into the triple-play totally redeemed himself with a spectacular two-strike bunt in the NCS quarterfinal game leading to the go ahead run in the bottom of the sixth. It just happened to be in the sixth game that we gave away last season.

That game and that season helped me to develop a better connection between mistakes and redemption, leading to a better *attitude* heading into this season. That approach has allowed the 2017 team to remain confident even after disappointment.

4th Inning

Top
Petersen – Strikeout
Armusewicz – Pop out to 1st base
Bentley – Single
Joyce – Fly out to right field
Bottom
Delst – Strikeout
Roth – Ground out to pitcher
Lance – Double, run scored
Hamilton – Single, RBI
McLaughlin – Pop out to 2nd base

All season long, there had been something about the 4th inning and this team. We usually did something cool and that was also when Jackie would fall asleep in the dugout during home games. Most of the time, we would have the lead when he woke up in the 7th. After two quick outs, our clean-up hitter hit a double and we were in business. Eamonn Lance was one of my three sophomore starters. At 5'11", 150 pounds, he might be small in stature but he had some juice. His work ethic was second to none. His family welcomed me into the community when I first moved to town in 2013. I lived in their pool house for six months, and I saw first-hand just how hard he worked, even as a seventh grader. He was the type of athlete that would do a five-mile run and then go take 300 swings and catch five bullpens. He had been one of our most consistent power threats, and now he was batting fourth for us in the MCAL Championship game and standing on second as Owen came to the plate.

After his two horribly unbalanced swings, I called time out. I could see his heart beating through his shirt as he jogged towards me. The crowd was standing, and all eyes were on us.

I could tell that he was feeling the weight of the moment. I put my hand on his chest and looked him in the eyes. It wasn't the first time I had seen him like this. Owen with no smile and jaws clenched was not his best approach. I told him to breathe, slow everything down, and enjoy the moment. The same thing that was written on our program standards poster hanging on our locker room wall all season long. I also told him to take the ball the other way and tie the game up. On the next pitch, that was exactly what he did. 1-1. We had a new ball game. Soft line drive over the second basemen's head, and just like that, he erased his error. That smile came back and all was right with the world again.

5th Inning

<u>Top</u>
Skinner – Fly out to center field
Harris – Base on balls
Castillo – Strikeout, Interference on steal attempt
<u>Bottom</u>
Clark – Strikeout
Brown – Fly out to center field
Leary – Hit by pitch
Delst – Strikeout

Our Rock

After an uncompetitive strikeout in the 5th inning, Rocky Clark pulled me to the side. He told me that he couldn't continue to play. After his first two at-bats, I could see that he was in a lot of pain. I wasn't going to play him, but before the game, he came to me and asked for a chance to be out there. Rocky was an appropriate name for the way his high school baseball career had gone. His real name was Connor and he didn't play baseball his freshman year. He was on the swim team. He was 5'10", 140 pounds, and water polo was his main sport for good reason. Drake had one of the best water polo programs in the country. The best athletes were in the water at our school. They went 29-1 in 2016 and were a perennial powerhouse that sent players on to play at college programs like Stanford and UC Davis.

Rocky decided to try out for baseball his sophomore season.

It was my last year at the JV level, and I fell in love with the way that he played the game. There was a toughness and passion in everything that he did, but he just couldn't stay healthy. He had elbow tendinitis from repetitive throwing in water polo and baseball. Radiating pain in wave-like surges all the way up his arm and into his upper shoulder made his elbow swell. He felt like his arm was going to fall off every time he threw. It didn't affect his bat, though. He was a designated hitter his sophomore season and was the heartbeat of our team when we won the 2015 MCAL JV championship. I will never forget what he showed me in our season ending, heartbreaking loss at MC that year.

The Bloody Game 2015

We were up 4-2 in the top of the 6th inning, getting ready to break it open. Rocky was up to bat with runners in scoring position. He was 2 for 2 already and really seeing the ball well. That was when a pitch came up and inside, right into his nose. He walked down to first base with blood gushing down his face.

I had to take him out of the game for obvious reasons, but he kept yelling, "I want to play," looking like a warrior deep in battle. The image is forever etched into my soul.

He couldn't play his junior year. He had a partial tear of the bicep tendon, making him completely unable to throw. He couldn't swing the bat either. The sharp pain was even affecting his sleep patterns. He came to me in the winter and told me that he wanted to play. He told me how important it was for him to be a part of this team his senior season. I didn't know what to expect out of him, but he was 6'1", 180 pounds of pure determination.

He started out on fire this season. He went 5 for 5 to start the season and was 12 for 28 (.428) before he had to stop playing for a while. Along with his tendinitis, he suffered from an allergic reaction to his acne medicine, and it caused very painful ingrown fingernails on both hands. His fingers would throb with sharp pain at even the slightest touch. It became painful for him to do everyday things like writing and giving handshakes. Swinging a baseball bat became excruciating to the point that he would sometimes vomit during batting practice.

Playing catch had become nearly impossible. It hurt when he threw, and it hurt when someone threw it to him. So when Rocky looked at me and said he couldn't go on, I knew that he had literally given his team everything that he had to give and more. I truly knew how badly he wanted to be out there on the field. As he stood in the dugout facing out to the field, I could see his teammates going to him with pats on the back and reassurances that we would win this game. Everyone knew how valuable Rocky was to the team.

The Redwood Rain Game

After a 12-0 start, it wasn't a coincidence that our first loss of the season was the first game that Rocky couldn't play. We were losing 1-0 at Redwood in the top of the 7th inning on a rainy afternoon. Eamonn drew a leadoff walk. Rocky asked if he could pinch hit and I let him. He hit a weak ground ball and the pitcher bobbled it. He dove head first into the base and beat out the throw, bad fingers and all. A pitch hit the next batter and the bases were loaded with nobody out.

The Redwood coach called time out and complained about the weather conditions. It was the same weather that they scored their run in the previous half inning. That was the same coach who looked me in the eyes before the game and said that we would play the game out, no matter what. And just like that, the game was called. They reverted to the 6th inning and, poof, the runners on the bases never existed. The game was over, and our winning streak had ended. It was our first bout with adversity and I would say we came out okay.

Winning streaks are misleading. We were not 12-0 good, but winning masks a lot of faults. That loss forced us to get better. Once we realized we weren't going undefeated for the season, we stopped worrying about our record and focused on playing good baseball.

The Redwood game also exposed my immaturity. I almost got myself fired because I lost sight of the importance of being a good human over all else. I threw a temper tantrum in the aftermath of the loss. It started during the game when the home plate umpire said he didn't like me. It seemed like Nick was getting squeezed and the Redwood pitcher was getting all the calls.

Honestly, I understand that the game needed to be called because the rain was getting too heavy. After the Redwood coach came out of the dugout to complain about the wet ball, both umpires walked off the field and sat in the Redwood dugout without saying anything to me. Redwood pulled their players off the field and our players stood on all three bases and in the batter's box. At that point, I began to take it personally.

Coach Will in the rain game

I thought umpires were supposed to communicate with both coaches before a decision was made, but I guess I was wrong.

After the game, my feelings were hurt. No umpire had ever told me that he didn't like me, and the way that the game ended made me angry. So I called my Athletic Director and complained and texted the head of umpires and asked that the home plate umpire from the Redwood game would not be allowed to do any more of our games. I let my emotions get the best of me when I was complaining to my AD and said some things that weren't true. I wanted to the hurt the umpire the way that I thought he'd hurt me, so I said that he had called me a "monkey" years ago.

In my small and selfish mind, I held the umpire solely responsible for ruining my chance at a perfect season, national coach-of-the-year honors, and a place in coaching immortality. When I said it, I just assumed that it would be something he would say because it fit my version of being wronged. I failed to realize that my AD was going to pursue my claims and make sure that we got to the bottom of this conflict with a peaceful resolution.

Between April 6 and May 2, 2017, my AD was the middleman in a "my word against his" dispute, based on a lie. Everything came to a head before our game vs. Branson and College of Marin when my AD set up a meeting between the umpire and me in the parking lot before the game.

I knew I was wrong. I just wanted this whole situation to go away, but it had already spiraled out of control and now I was about to be confronted face to face as the accuser.

Before he said a word, I could see the fury in his eyes. He told me about his family and one of the parents that raised him was African-American. He asked me to tell the truth and I couldn't. I was paralyzed in my lie and it was eating me alive. I couldn't sleep at all that night.

I was forced to face myself and truly reflect on my actions. I had to own it, just like I tried to teach my players whenever they made a mistake. My "poor loser" *attitude* after a little bit of failure in the Redwood game had turned me into the worst kind of person. I treated him the same way that I had been treated all my life. I looked at the color of his skin and made an immediate assumption that I knew what type of person he was. I lost of piece of myself and put a serious dent in my integrity.

I also realized that if I came clean at this point, I would most likely get fired and ruin the season for my players. I called Adam first thing in the morning and told him what was happening. I wanted to make sure that if I was let go that the team would have a coach moving forward toward the playoffs.

I sent an email to my Assistant Principal and AD telling them everything and I called the umpire and apologized for challenging his integrity. I didn't know what was going to happen and, with only four regular season games remaining, I was a nervous wreck.

Finally, a meeting was scheduled for the following week and I just knew it was the end for me. It was an integrity issue. The trust between my AD and me had been shattered and it was my fault. I held myself one hundred percent accountable for putting him in a truly messed-up situation.

On the day of the meeting, I received a text from the AD asking me something about next year and it kind of put me at ease. If they were going to take my keys and send me packing, I didn't think he would want my opinion about next year. Once again, it was baseball that saved me. Although the AD's initial response was to let me go, he explained to me the impact I had on the team and the program. He said that the issue was between us and had nothing to do with how I was as a coach.

I was grateful for his effort when he was sticking up for me. Both the Assistant Principal and AD commended me for telling the truth, even though they knew it could have cost me my job.

I appreciated the understanding from my AD and have made it a point to work hard to re-earn his trust. Our relationship was broken, and he still decided to stick with me. That said a lot about his character and I will forever be grateful for the way that he handled the situation.

More importantly, I received a great big hug from the umpire after the MCAL semifinal game. As we embraced, I was filled with regret. There was nothing that I could ever do to make up for the pain that I must have caused him while he held me tight and whispered words of encouragement.

They both wanted me to focus on finishing a great season. They recognized what type of team we had and wanted me to lead them. It was a special group that needed my attention. I could finally exhale a huge sigh of relief and get back to baseball.

6th Inning

Top
Petersen – Strikeout
Armusewicz – Ground out to 3rd base
Bentley – Single
Joyce – Fly out to right field

Bottom
Roth – Pop out to 2nd base
Lance – Fly out to right field
Hamilton – Pop out to 2nd base

7th Inning

Top
Caravello – Ground out to 3rd base
Mauterer – Ground out to shortstop
Skinner – Ground out to catcher

Bottom
McLaughlin – Strikeout
Woodrow – Ground out to shortstop
Brown – Fly out to left field

8th Inning

Top
Harris – Single
Castillo – Sacrifice bunt to pitcher
Petersen – Pop out to shortstop
Armusewicz – Fly out to left field

Bottom
Yamane – Ground out to 3rd base
Leary – Ground out to 3rd base
Delst – Ground out to shortstop

9th Inning

Top
Bentley – Fly out to center field
Joyce – Strikeout
Caravello – Ground out to catcher

Bottom
Roth – Base on balls
Lance – Base on balls
Hamilton – Sacrifice bunt to pitcher
McLaughlin – Base on balls
Woodrow – Strikeout

Brown – Strikeout

As the game went on, Ryan grew stronger on the mound. He was throwing harder than he was in the 1st inning and was pounding the zone with strike after strike. He finished with a bang. He sat MC down, 1-2-3, in his last inning of work. He went nine innings without giving up an earned run. He knew he was coming out and wanted to get the win.

The crowd appreciated his effort and rose to their feet. They began to chant, "I BELIEVE THAT WE WILL WIN, I BELIEVE THAT WE WILL WIN." This was the inning. It was time for a walk off. Looking around the dugout, I could feel it. What a great way to end it!

Nick led off the bottom of the 9th with a walk. Eamonn followed him and walked too. The crowd was beginning to swell. Owen laid down a perfect sacrifice bunt and now we had runners at second and third with one out.

MC intentionally walked Ryan to load the bases and turned the squeeze play into a force at home and not a tag. I thought about running the squeeze anyway, but I didn't pull the trigger and I am still kicking myself about it. Hindsight is always 20/20.

Eric struck out on a full count by swinging at ball four and Patrick struck out looking. The inning was over, the crowd was deflated, and, after two extra innings, neither team would budge.

Gallery B

Redwood baseball team hands Drake its first defeat

By Marin Independent Journal

POSTED: 04/06/17, 9:15 PM PDT | UPDATED: ON 04/07/2017

The Redwood High baseball team handed Drake its first loss of the season, winning 1-0 Thursday in a game shortened due to rain. The Pirates (12-1, 7-1 MCAL) loaded the bases with no outs in the top of the seventh inning, but the game was called and the Giants took home the victory.

Dane Goodman scored the Giants' (10-4, 7-1) lone run on a squeeze bunt as Nick Roth and Zach Tonnerre engaged in a pitchers' duel.

The Pirates topped San Rafael 3-2 on Tuesday behind Ryan McLaughlin's strong start (6 1/3 innings, three hits, eight strikeouts).

Tam picks up key win over first place Drake

By **Danny Schmidt**, *Marin Independent Journal*

POSTED: 04/25/17, 9:08 PM PDT | UPDATED: ON 04/26/2017

Tam High baseball coach Nathan Bernstein took no time in answering the question.

His Red-tailed Hawks had just beaten first-place Drake 3-2 in San Anselmo on Tuesday to remain in third place in the MCAL standings. The win was Tam's third straight.

So, of the dozen victories the Hawks (12-6, 8-4 MCAL) have recorded this season, where does Tuesday's rank?

"That is definitely the biggest win of the season," Bernstein said with a smile.

Tam entered the heavyweight matchup taxed after working overtime last week. The Hawks had nine- and ten-inning games sandwiched around a seven-inning win against Justin-Siena in their three games last week. With an exhausted pitching staff — and the next two hurlers due in the rotation unavailable — Sam Spiegelman made his second start of the season against the league's second-most potent offense.

The senior dazzled after allowing a first-inning run. He was taken out after four innings of three-hit ball in which he struck out two batters and walked one to earn the victory.

"Sam Spiegelman pitched the game of his life," Bernstein said. "I could not be happier. It's rare that things work out that nicely. Things weren't set up perfectly, but we just had to compete."

Ryan Leake, Tam's speedy right fielder, jumpstarted the offense within a minute of the first pitch. The leadoff batter belted a two-strike home run over the left-field fence in the first plate appearance of the game. Nicki Brass (2 for 3) and Will Muir each singled, and Jack Dickson's base hit resulted in Brass scoring — with the help of an outfield error — giving Tam a first-inning lead against Nick Roth, one of the county's premier pitchers.

"Roth is as good as you get in the league," Bernstein said. "We've now faced him four times in the last two years, so it was nice to finally get him. He pitched his butt off. He was phenomenal."

The Pirates (15-3, 10-2) cut the deficit in half in the bottom of the first when Gabe Leary drove in Jensen Yamane with two outs.

Pitching and defense were on display over the next five scoreless innings. Drake got runners on second and third in the bottom of the fifth, but Jack Loder, who tossed three relief innings, escaped the jam to preserve Tam's 2-1 lead.

The Hawks tacked on an insurance run in the top of the seventh but nearly added a few more. After Bennett Flynn reached on an error and Matt Kearney launched a hard single off the left- field wall, David Fineman came through with an RBI single up the middle. Leake was plunked, which loaded the bases, and Jacob Berg sent reliever Keegan Pedersen's pitch toward the gap in right-center. Right fielder Ryan McLaughlin made a highlight-reel diving catch and came up firing to third base, doubling up the runner and keeping the score within two runs.

Loder's only mistake of the game came in the bottom of the seventh against Case Delst, who drove a fastball over the wall in left field to trim Tam's lead to 3-2 with two outs. Loder, who pitched last Tuesday and Friday, needed one pitch after the homer to record the game's final out.

"I wasn't feeling it on the mound," a smiling Loder said regarding any arm pain. "I'll get it iced.

"I've pitched a lot against Drake the last couple years, and the key is...they're not going to make a lot of mistakes — they're a really well-disciplined team — so you have to pound the outside part of the plate and you can't give them anything. They don't give you much, so you have to make sure you're clean."

Roth, who entered the game with a 0.64 ERA, tossed six-plus innings, allowing one earned run on seven hits with three strikeouts. Delst reached in three of his four plate appearances, and Owen Hamilton and Eric Woodrow finished with two hits apiece.

"We hit a lot of balls right at people today," Drake coach Will Mosley said. "Offensively, we just couldn't catch any breaks. We played well enough to win, but it wasn't good enough today.

"They're a good team. They lost some tough games and they're going to be there in the end. It was a good MCAL game."

The Pirates' three losses have been by a combined three runs this season. They entered Tuesday's game with an unheralded team ERA of 0.48.

Drake faces Justin-Siena Friday in Napa, while Tam plays San Rafael at Albert Park.

"Like I told my guys, we lost one game in the first half (of the season) and one game in the second," Mosley said. "We're 10-2 with six games left; we're OK."

Redwood baseball tops Drake in extra innings

By Marin Independent Journal

POSTED: 05/09/17, 9:51 PM PDT | UPDATED: ON 05/09/2017

Redwood topped the cream of the MCAL crop on Tuesday, beating Drake 3-1 in nine innings for the second time this season. Anthony Pomilia, who recorded four hits for the Giants (14-9, 11-6), drove in two runs and Mackie Skall scored twice. Michael Benz pitched eight innings for Redwood, allowing one run on five hits with five strikeouts.

Case Delst (2 for 3, double, RBI), Patrick Brown (1 for 1, run) and Ryan McLaughlin (double) paced the Pirates' (19-4, 14-3) offense.

Chapter 3 – Effort

Effort: *a vigorous or determined attempt*
- Physical: Push yourself to the point of exhaustion.
- Mental: Strength and growth come only through continuous effort and struggle.

- Self-Check: Is this the most I can give?

7:00am

Just like clockwork, Jackie needed to go out just as I got to sleep for the first time. Finally, some REM sleep and his whining woke me. After he took more time than usual to do his business, I wasn't going back to sleep anytime soon.

The game was still six hours away and it had only been six hours since we stopped playing. I didn't know whether to be nervous or disappointed. Part of me was excited about still having a chance to win the championship and the other part was still pissed about how many chances we let get away.

I had to eat something. I was hungry, even though I tried to eat right after the game. There wasn't much open in San Anselmo after midnight, so we had to stop at Jack in the Box.

My Boy and I

My son, Jaheem, came to the game last night with his mother from Fairfield. It was the first time she had ever come to a Drake baseball game. When I promised to feed them after the game, I wasn't expecting it to be after midnight.

His mom texted me when they got home safely at 1:30am. She said she enjoyed herself and that the crowd was something out of *High School Musical*. According to her, even though the game was way too long, she was glad she and Jaheem had come. According to her, it was the best baseball game she had ever seen and had never experienced anything quite like it. Even though she didn't know any of the players, she still felt a connection with them after being there.

Jaheem was twelve years old and wanted to play at Drake. He had been around the program for seven years. He had been around baseball, swinging a bat and running bases from the time he could walk. He watched how hard the boys had worked and wanted to be there last night, even though he had a game the next day that he was beginning to warm up for right about now.

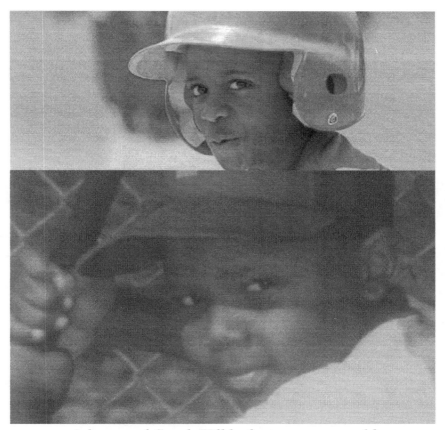

Jaheem and Coach Will both at seven years old

I hated that I had to miss my son's game that morning. I loved watching him play and baseball was a big part of our relationship. He absolutely loved the game and we had been able to spend a lot of time together on the field. Last summer, we did the four corners together. He played in Seattle, Los Angeles, New York, and Florida at eleven years old. He was a much different type of player than I was, but he played the game at a very high level for his age. I am looking forward to watching him grow. We exchanged good luck texts that morning. He was pitching against the first place team. He wanted to be here, and I wanted to be there, but, about twelve hours ago, the game started, and it still had a hold on me. No matter what I tried to do to distract myself, I kept reliving each moment. I could still hear the roars and groans of the crowd as the background music to my every thought.

One-Legged Pedersen

Keegan entered the game in the top of the 10th inning. He hobbled out to the mound with a "bad wheel," determined to put up a zero. He gave up a walk and a single, and no runs, thanks to a great catch by Isaac ranging from second base into shallow right field, barely avoiding a collision with Ryan, who was racing in from deep right. They both stayed down, but Isaac showed the ball to the umpire. As a 6'1", 165-pound sophomore, Isaac had become a defensive specialist. He had made several great and timely plays to preserve wins throughout the season.

Great defense in extra innings

I jogged out from the dugout to check on my players. Right next to me was Keegan, hopping on one leg, going to check on his teammates. I sent him to the dugout; everyone was okay and the game was still tied.

Keegan Pedersen pitching on one leg

If Nick was our emotional leader and Jensen was our analytical leader, then Keegan was our vocal leader. His body may have been failing him since the eighth grade, but his mind was a thing of beauty. He had the pulse of the team and I could trust him to keep them in the right thought pattern. He came complete with the shades, no shoes or maybe sandals on a good day. He was a super confident young man that could never stay healthy. It all started with a broken thumb in his last year of little league. He broke his thumb on his throwing hand in the championship game when he dove to tag a player at the plate. He was cleated, but he got the out. His coach had thought it was dislocated, so he tried to put it back. He managed to pitch three more innings and hit a one-handed double, but because of continuing to play that day, the original fracture grew from just the bottom thumb joint to grow to the connecting point of his wrist.

Freshman year, he broke the same thumb during football season but taped it up and played the rest of the year as a receiver. He also had two concussions but only reported one. After throwing 79.9 mph in the fall, he partially tore his UCL in his right arm in the last couple games of the baseball season.

Sophomore year, he broke two more fingers in football and had two more concussions. Thankfully, they kept him out and his head and fingers were able to heal. He made it through JV baseball somewhat healthy and was able to pitch and play outfield.

Junior year, he tore his LCL in his knee in football but managed to have a good baseball season out of the bullpen. He was 2-0 with 2.21 ERA with nine appearances, and he was one of the bright spots on the pitching staff. Voted a captain by his peers, this season, Keegan continued to fight the injury bug. At the beginning of the season, he was diagnosed with thoracic outlet syndrome. He started losing feeling in his hand after 15-20 pitches. After the first MC game to begin MCAL play, he tore a previously sprained ligament in practice and missed thirty-one days. His first bullpen back, he only threw four out of fifty strikes. He worked his way back on the mound and had been dynamite ever since. He came into last night with a record of 1-1 and only had given up one earned run in twelve innings of work.

He spent time with our top-notch trainer Andrew Blood every day. I was told several times that he could not do any more damage to the ankle, and like Rocky's hands, it was only about pain tolerance. We were very fortunate to have a quality trainer and we worked him overtime. He had kept our team stitched together with paper clips and duct tape, and as soon as Keegan returned to the dugout after the inning, his shoe was off, and Blood went to work on it. It was the bottom of the 10th and it was time for our offense to wake up. All we needed was one run. The *effort* was there.

10th Inning
Top
Mauterer – Strikeout
Skinner – Fly out to left field
Harris – Base on balls
Castillo – Single
Petersen – Fly out to right field
Bottom
Yamane – Strikeout
Leary – Single
McCaffrey – Pinch Runner, thrown out at home
Delst – Base on balls
Roth – Base on balls
Lance – Fly out to right field

Gabe, another one of the sophomores, got a one out single. He had a hard luck season in the leadoff spot.

At 6'2", 170 pounds, he hit the ball hard. This season, it just happened to be right at people. He had only played about eight games his freshmen season because of a broken foot but worked hard in the off-season to earn a spot on the varsity team. Now his run would win it in the 10th.

Case drew a walk, and I put in a pinch runner, Bryan McCaffrey, for Gabe at second base. Nick walked, and now we had the bases loaded for the second inning in a row. The crowd got back on their feet, ready to erupt as Eamonn came to the plate. He doubled and scored our only run of the game, way back in the 4th inning. Once again, I could have gone with the force play squeeze, but I didn't want to take the bat out of my clean-up hitter's hands.

He hit an extremely shallow fly ball that only went about fifteen feet past the infield dirt. Even though Owen was coming up to bat, like an idiot, I sent the runner from third base anyway. I wasn't sure what I thought was going to happen, but an eruption came from the MC fan section when Bryan was thrown out by at least ten steps.

Trigger Happy Coach

It wasn't the first time I froze and sent a runner to slaughter. In 2006, at the Perfect Game BCS Championship in Fort Myers, Florida, there had been no outs and I sent a runner from third in the top of the 1st inning against the Georgia Roadrunners.

The next batter hit a single. We ended up losing the game 1-0. My current JV coach, Anthony, was on that team. He hit a booming grand slam in the next game. I felt very lucky to have him on my staff. He brought a unique perspective to the program, having played for me as well as being my assistant coach with the 2014 Cooperstown championship team. Anthony always loved the game, and it showed on the field. He was part of a special group in 2006. It was my first elite team and they played the game at a very high level. The California Rebels were based out of Benicia. We practiced at Fitzgerald Field, and players came from as far as Cloverdale and never missed a workout.

2006 California Rebels 16U Roster

- *9 players received baseball scholarships from the following*

  schools: Cal State East Bay, Harris-Stowe University, University of Pennsylvania, Cal State Fullerton, Sonoma State, Oregon State, Naval Academy, UC Berkeley, Lewis-Clark University
- *Two players were drafted by and signed with the San Francisco Giants in 2010*

I blamed myself for losing that game and keeping the Rebels out of the championship bracket, because I got trigger-happy and sent a runner prematurely. I did it again tonight and that sinking feeling in my stomach came creeping back.

My blunder ended the rally and I wanted to go crawl in a hole somewhere. I wanted to win so badly that I panicked; something my team hadn't done all night. As I was doing the pace of shame back to the dugout, Keegan was putting his shoe back on, ready to go back out there and keep us tied. He smiled at me and said, "I got you, Coach" as everyone was privately asking Bryan if I sent him or did he go on his own. He was definitely following my orders and I sent him to a painful death in front of a packed house.

11th Inning

Top
Armusewicz – Strikeout
Bentley – Fly out to right field
Joyce – Fly out to center field
Bottom
Hamilton – Single
McLaughlin – Strikeout
Casey – Strikeout
Petersen - Strikeout

12th Inning

Top
Caravello – Base on balls, stolen base
Mauterer – Strikeout
Skinner – Single
Harris – Strikeout
Castillo - Strikeout
Bottom
Yamane – Single
Leary – Fielder's choice
Delst – Base on balls
Roth – Strikeout
Lance – Hit by pitch
Hamilton – Ground out to shortstop

Keegan had a 1-2-3 inning in the 11th, and I had a decision to make. His spot was coming up in the lineup and he couldn't run. I decided to stick with him, and all I can say is that he swung very hard three times. I didn't really have any other options, plus I needed one more inning out of him if I could get it. He walked the leadoff batter to start the 12th inning and I replaced him with Owen to a booming and well-deserved round of applause. Keegan limped off the field for the last time ever. He had given his team every ounce of *effort* he had.

Owen proceeded to strike out three of the next four batters and gave us yet another chance to get the walk-off hit. It was another chance to end this insanity and send the dedicated Drake fans home happy.

Nick trying to get the crowd going with sockless Keegan looking on

Jensen led off the bottom of the 12th with a single. Gabe hit into a fielder's choice and, with one out, Case drew a walk. Nick struck out and Eamonn reached base by a hit by pitch. Bases were loaded once again, for the third time in the last four innings. This time, it was two outs and I had no signs to give. I was hoping for passed ball, wild pitch, or an error. How many times would we not be able to score with a runner only ninety feet away? Owen had another chance to be the hero on a night when he accounted for the runs on both sides. The crowd was ripe with anticipation. A routine groundball to the shortstop and a perfect throw to first base ended in another disappointment.

13th Inning

Top

Petersen – Ground out to 2nd base

Armusewicz – Ground out to 2nd base

Bentley – Strikeout reached on dropped 3rd strike

Tarkenton – Ground out to 1st base

Bottom

McLaughlin – Base on balls

Friedenberg – Strikeout

Graves – Strikeout

Yamane – Ground out to shortstop

14th Inning

<u>Top</u>

Caravello – Single, caught stealing

Maderer – Strikeout

Skinner - Strikeout

<u>Bottom</u>

Leary – Single

Delst – Single

Roth – Bunt out to pitcher

Lance – Ground out double play to shortstop

Owen continued to shut them down and we continued to start rallies and not finish them. In the bottom of the 14th, Gabe led off with a single, followed by another single from Case. With runners on first and second and nobody out, Nick laid down a bad bunt right back to the pitcher and he was able to get the lead runner at third. Then Eamonn hit into a 6-4-3 double play. Another promising inning was over just like that.

15th Inning

<u>Top</u>

Harris – Pop out to 3rd base

Castillo – Ground out to pitcher

Petersen – Fly out to center field

<u>Bottom</u>

Hamilton – Base on balls, stolen base

McLaughlin – Strikeout

Friedenberg – Strikeout

Graves – Hit by pitch

Yamane – Base on balls

Leary – Line out to 2nd base

Owen cruised through the top of the 15th and gave us another chance to see how close we could get to finally winning the game but fall short. It had been a recurring theme from the 9th inning on. Owen led off the inning with a walk, and stole second base. Ryan and Isaac had back-to-back strikeouts, and Spencer Graves, who entered the game for Keegan in the 12th, reached base by a hit by pitch. Jensen drew a walk, and the bases were full of Pirates for the umpteenth time. Gabe had a great at-bat and smashed a ball the other way. There just happened to be an MC player right there on the other end of the line drive. Off the bat, it looked good, but it was quickly caught, and another three men were stranded on base.

16th Inning

<u>Top</u>

Armusewicz – Single
Bentley – Pop out to catcher
Tarkenton – Ground out double play to shortstop
<u>Bottom</u>
Delst – Pop out to shortstop
Roth – Hit by pitch
Lance – Fly out to right field
Hamilton – Pop out to shortstop

17th Inning

<u>Top</u>
Caravello – Reached on 1st base error
Mauterer – Fielder's choice
Skinner – Ground out to shortstop
Harris – Base on balls
Castillo – Ground out to 1st base
<u>Bottom</u>
McLaughlin – Single, caught stealing
Friedenberg – Fly out to right field
Graves – Ground out to 3rd base

18th Inning

<u>Top</u>
Petersen – Single
Armusewicz – Ground out double play to shortstop
Bentley – Fly out to center field
<u>Bottom</u>
Yamane – Fly out to center field
Leary – Fly out to left field
Delst – Ground out to shortstop

Owen ran into a bit of trouble in the top of the 17th. MC got a runner to third base with two outs. It was only their third runner to get that far all game. He was able to get a groundout and end the threat. In the 16th and 18th innings, our infield defense turned sweet double plays right before and after the midnight hour. Owen pitched seven scoreless innings in relief, and in between innings, he received treatment from Blood for a stiff back.

Our catcher was the hardest working player on the field.

Case caught 233 pitches with no passed balls. He saved at least two runs with great blocks and worked miracles with the pitching staff. Case wasn't a fan of Albert Park. He felt the lights were too dim and I agreed. Earlier in the year, he had a bit of a meltdown the first time we played under the lights, but tonight, he was a total stud. He had been on the varsity team since his freshman year and was the starting third basemen on the 2015 NCS Championship team. Catching was his third position in three years, after playing first base last year. He was the only non-senior captain and had earned the respect of his teammates because of nights like this. After eighteen innings in a squat, I wasn't sure just how much longer he could go. Thankfully, time was on his side.

Due to the San Rafael city ordinance that does not allow any new inning to begin after midnight, the league officials called the game. Exhausted players, umpires, and fans emptied the ballpark last night, realizing they were part of something special.

It had been decided that the game would resume at 1:00pm at Drake the next day. My first thought had been *What in the world am I going to do for the next eleven hours?*

Gallery C

Act I: Drake-Marin Catholic called after 18 innings; MCAL title to be decided Saturday

*By **Danny Schmidt**, Marin Independent Journal*

POSTED: 05/20/17, 1:07 AM PDT | UPDATED: ON
05/20/2017

Five hours and 10 minutes — or 18 innings if you prefer — is typically enough time to play a pair of high school baseball games.

But the MCAL championship game between No. 1 Drake and No. 2 Marin Catholic, which began at 7 p.m. Friday and was called just after midnight Saturday, is still going.

The rival baseball teams put on a remarkable show for a raucous crowd that remained near capacity throughout the 18-inning marathon at Albert Park.

Officials called the 1-1 game, which will resume from the top of the 19th inning at 1 p.m. Saturday at Drake.

With runs and hits at a premium — per usual in the MCAL — the thought of extra innings was prevalent, especially within the Marin Independent Journal sports department.

Marin Catholic (14-10) struck first, scoring one run in the top of the second inning on an RBI sacrifice fly from Vaughn Mauterer, who plated Taylor Bentley. The Pirates (20-5) knotted the score at 1-1 in the fourth when Eamonn Lance narrowly beat the tag at home plate on Owen Hamilton's RBI single to right field.

Then came the zeroes.

But the game was anything but dull. The crowd remained lively with ample back-and-forth chants well into the night. When the announcement was made the game would soon be called,
Drake's student section began hollering for another inning.

Drake had numerous opportunities to score, but could not get the winning run across. From the eighth inning to the 15th, the Pirates stranded 13 runners, failing to score with the bases loaded in multiple frames.

Dylan Joyce and Ryan McLaughlin were stellar for their respective teams, each going eight-plus innings on the mound. Drake's Owen Hamilton and Keegan Pedersen and Marin Catholic's Sean Henry, Mauterer, Hayden Wellbeloved and Jack Hurley all tossed scoreless relief innings.

Gabe Leary, who made his ninth and final plate appearance in the 18th inning at 12:05 a.m., went 2 for 5 in extra innings alone. Hamilton and Jensen Yamane also recorded multiple hits for the Pirates, as did Marin Catholic's Nick Caravello (3 for 6, walk).

Both teams will likely earn favorable seeds for the North Coast Section playoffs, which begin next week, assuming the league title has been won by then.

Chapter 4 – Endurance

Endurance: *an ability or strength to continue or last, especially despite fatigue, stress, or other adverse conditions*

- Physical: Train your body to finish practices, games, and season with force.

- Mental: Tough times don't last; tough people do. Your struggles develop your strengths.

- Self-Check: Do I really want to give up now??

10:00am

Walking from the car the to the field, I had a feeling of hopeful uncertainty. I truly didn't know what to expect from the guys, but we were back home at our field. One of the luxuries of being the #1 seed of the MCAL tournament was hosting the continuation of the championship game at our place, because the more spacious Albert Park was not available. The game wouldn't begin for another three hours, but I just had to get out of the house. The players wouldn't be there for a while, but I could already feel the butterflies in my stomach. I just sat in the dugout, looking out at the field. There was nothing for me to do. The lineup was set from last night. We were down to our last pitcher and our catcher just squatted for five hours. Spencer would get the ball. He was 3-0 with fifteen innings and had only given up one earned run. There were no strategies or scouting reports to go over. I was interested in finding out if we still had any "gas left in the tank." I could give the "win or lose, I'm still proud of them" speech, but they would see right through that. I had no idea what to say that hadn't already been said in the previous eighteen innings. As the players began to arrive, I soon realized that I wouldn't have to say anything at all. The mood felt right. There was a level of loose focus that relaxed me right away. It was just what I was looking for.

We decided to take an abbreviated infield/outfield and it was flawless. Players had a bounce in their step, throws were perfect, and no one dropped a ball. It was quick and precise. MC looked like they had just played eighteen innings. Their infield was sloppy and without any energy.

Our players saw this and continued to build confidence as the fans filled the bleachers and overflowed into the walkways. It was by far the most fans I'd ever seen at a baseball game at Drake before.

Spencer was all set to go for the top of the 19th. He struck out the first batter, but then Nick made an error on a groundball to third base. The runner advanced to second base on a wild pitch. With the go-ahead run on second base, Spencer was able to get the next hitter to fly out to center field for the second out. Then, he struck out the last batter to end the inning and send us into the bottom of the 19th, tied at 1-1.

Nick led off the inning with a hard groundball to shortstop for the first out. Eamonn hit a soft liner off the end of the bat for the second out. We made two outs on four pitches, and it was up to Owen to extend the inning, or at least make the pitcher work a little bit. He took the first pitch for a strike and looked at me, giving a head nod. He took the second pitch for a ball. The next pitch, he met very well. As soon as he connected, the whole place exploded. As the ball sailed over the fence, everything was in slow motion.

When the ball landed beyond the wall, the whole place erupted with an enormous roar. The players made a mad dash for the plate and I was stuck in that place between reality and a dream.

Parents who I had never seen smile were jumping out of their seats with their hands raised. The players were up against the fence with anticipation while the MC players lowered their heads. Some of them squatted or fell to the ground.

I saw Owen's huge smile coming around second base and broke into a dance. As he passed third, he slapped my hand on the way by. He tossed his helmet to the sky and received his hero's welcome at home plate. I let out a deep sigh of relief and absolute madness ensued. Parents and fans ran onto the field and it was all a blur.

I did a little celebration dance as the entire stadium swelled with excitement. Everyone had just *endured* a roller coaster of a game with a storybook ending. I was as high as I had ever been on a baseball field. It was a feeling like none other.

There were so many happy faces jumping around looking for someone to hug, but I had one more thing to do. I made sure a couple of his teammates kept him distracted, and I gave Owen the Gatorade bath of his life. He never saw it coming and it was cold, but Owen Hamilton had just hit a walk-off. He was floating on Cloud 9 and didn't feel a thing.

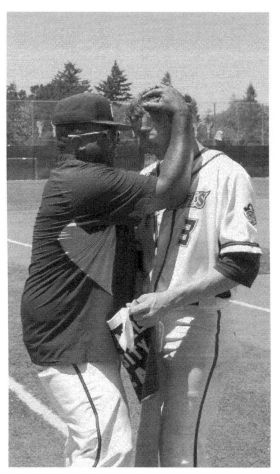

Coach Will and Owen sharing a special moment

We waited eleven hours for fifteen minutes of baseball. Fans were still walking in from the parking lot as Owen was rounding the bases. Dozens of people came up to us as we were leaving the field, saying they just missed it but were following the game on Twitter. Apparently, the game had quite a following. Video highlights from the game were all over the place. Max Preps, *USA Today*, and NBC Sports featured the walk-off home run filmed by Danny Schmidt from the *Marin Independent Journal*.

MCAL Tournament Champions

I received dozens of texts and congratulatory messages on social media immediately after the game. It was surreal. We had just won the MCAL Championship, went nineteen innings, didn't give up an earned run, and won on a walk-off homerun. While the team was having a party that evening, I was back out at the field with my son, four hours after the game. I love throwing to him for batting practice, and he loves to hit at Drake. He told me about his game and I told him about mine. It was a perfect ending to a great day.

Jaheem getting his work in as the sun goes down

As wonderful as the win was, now I had to figure out how to focus myself and the team on our first-round North Coast Section game next week. I guess this was a good problem to have, but I believed there was going to be some sort of hangover. At Monday's practice, the team might as well have been wearing khaki shorts, flip-flops, and Hawaiian shirts. We got absolutely no work done. I had to ban any further talk of the game at all practices. It was a major distraction and, if we had to play on Tuesday, we would have lost badly. Thankfully, we didn't play until Wednesday. That extra day was invaluable. We needed more time for some of our players to descend back to earth.

Tuesday's practice put things back in focus with drill work. We prepared for our first-round NCS game with defensive situations, baserunning and had a good batting practice.

NCS Round #1
May 24th, 2017

We played the #14 seed Bishop O'Dowd and they came to win. They scored a run in the 1st inning and another one in the third off Nick. His ball was flat, and he didn't have any legs. Our bats were sluggish through the zone and O'Dowd was bringing the energy. We were down 2-0 going into the bottom of the 5th inning. Honestly, there were probably a whole lot of people that would've been okay with a loss today under those circumstances. Not being able to bounce back with another win wouldn't diminish the great season or take away the epic championship. However, this team had one more banner to get. At the beginning of the season, they set out to win the regular and post-season MCAL titles and the Division 3 NCS title, and all our goals were still intact.

Gabe led off the inning with a fly out to center. Case hit a single to left. Nick flew out to right. Eamonn doubled off the fence and we had runners on second and third with two outs.

Owen was the right man in the right spot. Everyone on the team was anticipating something great, and he delivered again. Off the bat, it looked and sounded like a three-run homerun, but it hit the top of the fence, and the game was tied 2-2. An immediate sense of comfort came over the team. Players walked around, telling each other they had been here before. It was interesting to see their level of confidence as the game went into extra innings, not in a cocky way, but very matter of fact about it.

Eric Woodrow led off the bottom of the 8th inning with an opposite field homerun, and we won, 3-2. I did the same dance, but my heart wasn't in it. Don't get me wrong, I was super excited, but the dance was now choreographed, not the same as a spontaneous boogie. I was happy for Eric. He struck on a pitch up and away with the bases loaded and a chance to win it in the MCAL Championship and worked on hitting that pitch in practice. He hit his first opposite field homerun in practice the day before he hit an opposite field walk-off home run in the bottom of the 8th. At this point, it felt like this team was destined to win it all. They had won back to back postseason games with extra inning walk-off homeruns. The team was doing some truly amazing things and I was incredibly excited to see what was going to happen next.

Eric Woodrow hit his 1st opposite field home run of his career

Welcome home Eric

Coach Will and Eric sharing a special moment

NCS Quarterfinals May 26th, 2017

We played the #6 seed Moreau Catholic for the second time this season. We beat them 2-1 in our first game of the season back in February. This time, it was quite a bit different. We scored two runs in the bottom of the first. Case hit a triple down the right field line to start things off. Nick, Eamonn, and Eric all hit singles and Owen walked. It felt nice to have a lead before the end of the game. We were winning 3-0 going into the bottom of the 6th, when Moreau ran out of pitchers, and we took full advantage. Four walks, three hit by pitch, and a grand slam by Owen sealed the deal on a 10-0 win. It was technically a six-inning mercy rule walk-off.

Owen met at home after another grand slam

It was a complete team win. Ryan threw a complete game and was masterful on the mound. We didn't make any errors, and we sprayed the ball around the park. Also, Owen did something cool again at our last home game of the year. We were two wins away from our final goal with our toughest two games of the season on the horizon. We would be on the road the rest of the way.

NCS Semifinals May 31st, 2017

We played the #2 seed Analy. They were riding a nineteen-game winning streak, and we were on that list. They gave us our second loss of the season during Spring Break. It was the first game after our six-inning loss with bases loaded in the top of the seventh game. We were still recovering from losing our twelve-game winning streak. The first time we met, we hadn't played well at all and lost 3-2 at their field with no outfield fences where their outfielders could play as deep as they wanted. There weren't going to be any homeruns in this game.

This time around, I was expecting a good old-fashioned pitchers' duel, and the game didn't disappoint. The score was 0-0 going into our lucky inning number four, and one of the craziest baseball plays I had ever seen gave us a 1-0 lead. Case doubled to lead off the top of the 4th. Nick moved him to third with a sacrifice bunt. I continued my non-squeeze approach and let Eamonn swing away. He drew a walk and Owen came to the plate. In the scorebook, he got credited with a sacrifice fly, but it was something altogether different. Owen hit a line drive rocket up the middle. Off the bat, it looked like it would fall just behind second base, so Case took off for home. The ball had so much backspin that it carried right to the centerfielder, giving Case no chance to tag up. That was until the centerfielder decided to throw the ball to first base, trying to double off Eamonn. The only problem with that was that his first baseman was in the center of the infield, setting up for the cut to home. The ball banged up against the first base dugout fence and Case was able to jog home for the 1-0 lead. Case claimed he went back and tagged up, but I didn't believe him. All that mattered was that we got our one run. The way that Nick was throwing the ball that day, it was all we needed. We also received a little more help from the Analy centerfielder.

Nick was cruising along, until the bottom of the 6th inning.

With one out, the centerfielder blasted a ball down the right field line headed toward the bullpen. He raced around first and slid headfirst into second. He stood up and started dusting himself off before he realized that Ryan had not even picked up the ball yet, after literally kicking it three times. He finally ran to third base as we got the ball back into the infield. If he had stayed on his feet, the game would have been undoubtedly tied 1-1. Granted, Ryan did throw a runner out at second on a backhand rocket throw in the 2nd inning. The runner was visibly shaken, but they still had a chance to tie with only one out. Even when Nick hit the next batter, the runner at third was still beating himself up, but they were in business. This was their best chance to score. Nick had other ideas as he struck out their third batter on a full count change-up, and the clean-up hitter on three pitches. He followed that up with a perfect 7th, and we were heading to the "ship."

After the final out, I met Nick coming off the field with a big hug and thanked him for giving everything he had in his last high school start. He gave up four hits and had ten strikeouts.

He was poised and dominant, and I was proud.

Coach Will and Nick sharing a special moment

We were going to the NCS Championship game in my second year as head coach, and with this win, we broke the school record for most wins in a season with twenty-four. Rick Lafranchi came up and shook my hand and congratulated me after the game. He had coached the Drake baseball team for over twenty years, so his words really meant a lot.

The wild ride continued with all our goals still intact, twenty-nine games into the season. We scheduled our program banquet for June 1st at the beginning of the year, hoping that we would still have one game to play.

2017 Drake Baseball Banquet
June 1st, 2017

The same thing happened in 2015. We had our banquet the night before the NCS Championship game and that worked out well for us. I liked it because I knew I wouldn't get too mushy knowing it wouldn't be the last time I saw the boys. We had more business to take care of. I really enjoyed banquets. I felt it was the best time to give thanks and show appreciation to everyone, no matter the size of their role on the field. I learned a while ago that a team is only as good as the type of players they have on the bench. I'd seen a lot of very talented teams ripped apart from the inside by one or more players unhappy with their role. My first year at Drake, I was told that I was the worst coach in America by a mother of a disgruntled player at the end-of- the-season banquet. I knew some guys wanted to play more, but they never let their disappointment with my decisions get in the way of doing what they needed to do to help the team.

Coach Will and the captains

I was very proud of the bench players, but especially Matt.

He had the most power on the team and had improved drastically from his sophomore year, but he just never could consistently break into the starting lineup. I started him in the nineteen-inning game and took him out of the game after he struck out in his first at-bat. He could have pouted and felt sorry for himself, but he didn't. He put his helmet on every time that his spot in the lineup came up, ready to re-enter if called upon. I respected people like that. One of the most difficult things to do in team sports is to be on the bench, watching your teammates play. Our bench was outstanding and showed a lot of character all season. All year long, I used a designated hitter for Ian and Isaac. They didn't let their offensive struggles or the fact that someone else was hitting for them affect their defense one bit.

Bryan was our pinch running specialist. He took it upon himself to study the craft of running the bases and embraced the role of scoring an important run late after not playing all game. Then you have Ryder. His high school battle made Rocky and Keegan look like crybabies. He beat leukemia and was one of the strongest kids I knew. Although he didn't play an inning, he was still a valuable member of our team. He grew up playing with the other nine seniors and had been a part of the journey all four years. Just having him with us forced the other players to suck it up when they were down, because nothing they experienced on the field could ever compare to his fight with cancer.

Finally, I thanked my staff for putting up with me. Kevin and Hoss were with me all season and played a vital part to our success. Good coaches with positive energy and integrity are hard to find. Kevin was new to the program this year and the players loved him immediately. He played at Washington State University and brought a ton of knowledge and passion to our program. Hoss had been at Drake for a long time. His two sons played for and graduated from Drake. We are lucky that he decided to stick around. He brought experience and had a wonderful connection with the players.

NCS Championship
June 3rd, 2017

There were only two scenarios that lead to a team knowing when their last practice is. Either your team didn't make the playoffs or you were in the championship. I definitely preferred the latter.

Our team had done everything that it set out to do up to this point, and the tone at practice reflected that. After getting a detailed scouting report on our opponent, we went to work. It wasn't a time for sentiments. The focus was real. Before they put their hands in for the last practice break of the season, I told them that all we had to do was score four runs and we would be NCS Champions.

We played the #1 seed, Miramonte. They were 27-0 and had just beaten Campolindo 11-1 in their semifinal game. The championship game was to be played at St. Mary's College in Moraga. We literally had to pass the Miramonte campus on the way to the game.

Their coach was retiring, and the team was dedicating the season to him. They were "big news" and this was the match-up I had hoped for. I had wanted to play them from the time that we were both 12-0 back in March. They ended our season a year ago and, even though I had met him several times, their coach kept reintroducing himself to me. I wanted him to remember me this time.

I told the players to arrive at the field an hour earlier than usual. I wanted them to get the lay of the land, to try and get comfortable in their surroundings, and to shake out any jitters. I let them take pictures, goof around, and share on social media. I wanted them to enjoy the moment. I had no doubt that they would be ready to play. We had been on a baseball high and were not ready to come down yet. I could see it in their eyes. I could tell by the way they were walking around that they were dialed in.

Team photo before NCS Championship Game

When Miramonte arrived at the normal time and saw us all settled in, they began to rush as if they were late. Our players gained confidence from watching them warm up. We sized them up and came to the collective conclusion that they were beatable. We even had more fans than they did. The bleachers were packed with Pirate fans, both young and old. They wanted to see if we could continue this amazing run and bring home the banner.

The Pirate fans packed the stands at St. Mary's College

We got on the board in the top of the 1ˢᵗ inning. Case hit a one out double and moved to third on a passed ball. Nick laid down perfect squeeze bunt and we were in the lead 1-0. We fell apart a bit in the bottom of the 3ʳᵈ inning. Ryan got a little shaky and literally dropped the ball while on the rubber, with a runner on third base. That was how Miramonte tied the game and took the lead on an error by Owen. Miramonte got two quick outs in the top of the 4ᵗʰ inning, and our bats came alive. Nick and Owen hit singles. Eric and Ryan hit doubles, and we took the lead 4-2 with a big two-out rally. Ryan ran into big trouble in the bottom of the 6ᵗʰ inning. Miramonte had bases loaded and nobody out. We pitched out on the first pitch to sniff out a squeeze and they were only able to scratch out one run on a sacrifice fly after a couple of big time strikeouts. With one out and a runner on first base in the bottom of the 7ᵗʰ, Ryan had reached his pitch limit. This was his last batter. For some strange reason, the runner tried to steal second base, and Case threw him out by a mile. There were two outs and no pitching change was necessary. With a ground out to Isaac, the game was over.

A dog pile ensued and I thought about participating for zero seconds. It looked like a lot of fun. Once the dog pile broke up, it happened. I knew it was coming, but I still couldn't get away. I tried to duck and do some sort of move from the *Matrix*, but they got me. Ice cold water down my back. I looked around at the players and the crowd with my soggy bottom and it hit me. We did what we set out to do in spectacular fashion in front of our family and friends. Most of these players had been playing together since t-ball, and now they had won it all together.

Coach Will watching the Dogpile

Coach Will with ice down his back

I couldn't help but giggle as they handed me the championship plaque and banner to a standing ovation.

I felt a great deal of jubilation. It was the kind of excitement that resulted in grown men jumping around hugging each other like elementary school kids. I was so excited for my seniors. There was no better way to end your high school career. As I placed the championship medals around each player, I followed it up with a great big hug and heartfelt congratulations. There was so much joy in their eyes and a sense of accomplishment radiated from them all.

Coach Will with the NCS Championship Banner and Plaque

Players paying tribute to the Pirate fans

NCS Division 3 Champions

Our celebration was cut short because they had to get the field ready for the De la Salle vs. Monte Vista Division I game. As we were leaving the field, the starting catcher for De la Salle came up and gave me a congratulatory hug and I wished him luck in his game. That player was Austin Elder. He was the kid that I started doing lessons with when he was five years old, in his own little backyard ballpark. He was headed to Cal State Northridge on a baseball scholarship. Baseball is such a small world.

When I finally had the chance to speak to my team alone, I realized that I didn't have anything else to say. What could I say? They answered the bell every time. They gave people something to cheer for and did it with flair. The only other time I was rendered speechless was after the California Daredevils won the Cooperstown National Championship in 2014. The crazy coincidence was that our three-year championship reunion party was scheduled for today, and here I was getting all choked up again. Baseball is amazing. I just looked at them and smiled. I shook my head in disbelief as the players repeated what I said at practice the day before. They told me that we still had all our goals intact, with no games to play, and all they had to do was score four runs. I just stood there and smiled.

I went home to pick up Jackie and headed to a beautiful home in Tiburon for the Daredevil reunion. Jackie and I entered the house to another standing ovation. They all had been following the game and season, even though none of them went to Drake.

Coach Will with the 2014 Cooperstown Champs

It was a joyous day for me. I was blessed enough to win a new championship and celebrate an old one on the same day. Saturday, June 3, 2017 was easily one of the best days of my coaching life.

Wouldn't you know it? Ten days later, our team was invited to the San Anselmo Town Council meeting on Tuesday, June 13th, to receive a Proclamation from the Mayor for our achievement. The Town Manager, Dave Donery, called it a "Huge historical MCAL moment." I tend to agree with him.

...All goals still intact!

Gallery D

Drake tops Marin Catholic behind Owen Hamilton's walk-off HR in 2-day, 19-inning MCAL title game

By **Danny Schmidt***, Marin Independent Journal*

POSTED: 05/20/17, 7:55 PM PDT | UPDATED: ON
05/21/2017

Well, that was fun.

It took two days — 19 innings played over the course of five hours and 20 minutes — six umpires, nine pitchers and a change in both location and climate. Fittingly, one swing lifted the top-seeded Drake High baseball team to a thrilling 2-1 victory against No. 2 Marin Catholic on Saturday in the MCAL championship game.

With two outs in the bottom of the 19th inning, Owen Hamilton sent a 1-1 fastball over the left-field fence — the sound of the ball meeting metal leaving no doubt — for a walk-off home run that put an exclamation point on a game that will live on in Marin County lore.

"I knew it was out right when I hit it," said Hamilton, who removed and lofted his helmet as he was mobbed at home plate. "At first it didn't feel like it was actually happening. As the ball was leaving the yard, everything felt so easy. This whole struggle of this long game finally came down to one easy swing, and it was hard to believe for me."

The marathon game between the league's top teams began at 7p.m. on Friday at Albert Park. The rivals carried a 1-1 tie from the fourth inning all the way into the 18th. Officials called the game at that point, minutes after the clock struck midnight, declaring action would resume on a sun-drenched Saturday afternoon at Drake.

Beginning in the top of the 19th, Marin Catholic's (14-11) Nick Caravello reached on an error — just the second of the game — and advanced to second base on a wild pitch. But Spencer Graves, Drake's (21-5) fourth pitcher of the game, induced a shallow fly ball and recorded an inning-ending strikeout, his second of the frame.

After a pair of quick outs, Hamilton, who was stellar in his seven-inning relief stint Friday (six strikeouts, one walk), made his ninth plate appearance with one objective: end the game.

The College of Marin-bound senior delivered, crushing his third homer of the season just 10 minutes after the sequel was underway.

"It's somewhat fitting that Owen was the one who got it done for them because of the way he finished the game last night," Marin Catholic coach Jesse Foppert said of Hamilton, who solely played designated hitter last spring due to an elbow injury. "He's a good kid and he's put in a lot of hard work."

Despite Drake loading the bases three times in extra innings — stranding 14 total runners in the final 10 innings — and coming within one ball of capturing the title in the bottom of the ninth, the game came down to a two-out, solo home run in the friendly confines of Drake's ballpark, an established hitter's field.

"Baseball's like music," Drake senior Keegan Pedersen said. "There are little lulls and then there will be a crescendo out of nowhere. But, hey, that's why everybody plays baseball."

Pitching from both sides was outstanding Friday, led by starters Dylan Joyce and Ryan McLaughlin. Joyce, a sophomore who entered the night with just 8 2/3 innings of work on the mound this spring, tossed eight innings of four-hit ball, allowing one run with seven strikeouts and no walks. McLaughlin, a junior, scattered three hits over nine innings, striking out four batters and walking one.

The Wildcats struck first in the second inning on a Vaughn Mauterer sacrifice fly that scored Taylor Bentley. The Pirates evened the score at 1-1 in the fourth when Eamonn Lance narrowly beat the tag at home plate on Hamilton's RBI single to right field.

Then Albert Park grew darker, with nothing but zeroes illuminating the scoreboard in right field.

Drake repeatedly had runners in scoring position, much to the delight of the school's student section, which, along with Marin Catholic, remained nearly at capacity throughout the 18-inning first act. The Pirates loaded the bases in the ninth, and Marin Catholic reliever Sean Henry worked a 3-2 count with the winning run 90 feet away. Henry escaped the jam with a pair of strikeouts. The Pirates had at least one runner reach base in all but one of the 12 extra innings.

"It was like one long dream-nightmare," Pedersen said. "Every inning was a roller coaster, every inning was something new. We came up with a million ways not to score. I can't explain it.

"I'm just proud of everybody here. It's the best feeling in the world."

Marin Catholic — the reigning MCAL champions and winners of its last seven games entering the final — had its chances, too, stranding a pair of runners in the top of the 10th and another two in the 12th.

But pitching and defense ruled. Following Joyce's start, Mauterer, Hayden Wellbeloved and Jack Hurley were solid out of the bullpen. The Pirates, whose staff lowered its exceptional 0.60 ERA, got strong innings from Pedersen and Hamilton. In addition to Hamilton, who had three, Gabe Leary — whose ninth plate appearance came at 12:05 a.m. Saturday — Jensen Yamane and Caravello all recorded multiple hits.

"It honestly feels like a 16-hour game," Pedersen said. "Everybody says that they got some sleep, but I guarantee they were up until 3 in the morning thinking about this moment. I got maybe two hours and I've had four Red Bulls in the last 24 hours.

"Our home crowd was amazing. In four years at Drake, I've never experienced that in any sporting event. The only thing that can calm down the nerves is the love everybody has for the team. I'm so proud of every single person on this team."

As players and coaches shook hands at home plate, the crowd offered a lengthy standing ovation. Following postgame team meetings, Marin Catholic coaches and players sat in the dug-out, watching as their counterparts celebrated with hugs, photos with the pennant and a Gatorade bath for Drake coach Will Mosley.

Senior Jack Harris, who led the Wildcats to the championship game with a dominating pitching performance in the semifinals, remained seated long after his teammates left, continuing to gaze onto the diamond.

"He really cares," Foppert said of Harris. "He puts his heart and soul into every minute he's on the baseball field, so he's going to take it hard.

"It was great to see the way both teams fought all last night and how they came back with the energy they had today. I'm very proud of our guys. Obviously you'd rather be on the other side of it, but it was definitely a fun game to be a part of."

Though the game felt like a track meet, Drake players ended their day in the pool, taking a victory dip in the 90-plus-degree weather before cleaning the field.

Both teams will likely earn favorable seeds in the North Coast Section playoffs. Brackets are released Sunday, with first-round games beginning Tuesday, assuming the teams recover by then.

"That win epitomizes our season," Mosley said. "I played 17 different players, threw four different pitchers and we gave up zero earned runs in 19 innings. To not give up an earned run in 19 innings against the hottest team, that's what our team is about. That's what we've been doing all year — it's not a fluke. That's what makes me comfortable in tight games — it's really hard to score on us.

"That was the best, most well-played game I've ever been a part of. All I can really say is how proud I am of these guys. They earned every single thing. And we still have one more to get."

Boys prep of the week: Owen Hamilton

POSTED: 05/22/17, 4:54 PM PDT | UPDATED: ON 05/22/2017

What he did: The College of Marin-bound senior ended a two- day, 19-inning MCAL championship game with a walk-off home run that powered Drake to a 2-1 victory against Marin Catholic. Hamilton — who had a hit, a walk and a run in the semifinals — pitched seven scoreless relief innings against MC on Friday night.

What he said: "It was crazy because it felt so easy. The whole 19-inning game had been so difficult and long, a great fight by both sides — Marin Catholic was a very, very determined
team — so when the game ended abruptly with that home run, it was hard to believe. It was very exciting. It's been a happy few days."

What's next: No. 3 Drake (21-5) hosts No. 14 Bishop O'Dowd (8-16) in the first round of the North Coast Section Division III playoffs.

— Danny Schmidt

"Owen's worked really hard. He loves baseball and he's dedicated himself. For him to do that against MC, who he's had trouble against, was spectacular."

Will Mosley: Drake coach on Hamilton, a second-team all-league selection.

Dramatic Drake walks off again

By Susanna Pilkerton, IJ correspondent

POSTED: 05/24/17, 10:00 PM PDT | UPDATED: ON 05/24/2017

The crowd was on its feet as junior Eric Woodrow rounded the bases after his walk-off solo home run in the bottom of the eighth. The blast propelled the No. 3 Pirates to a 3-2 win over No. 14 Bishop O'Dowd in the first round of the North Coast Section Division III tournament. The win comes less than a week after Drake's two-day, 19-inning win against Marin Catholic in the MCAL championship.

Coming off of last weekend's game, Drake felt comfortable going into the extra inning tied at 2-2, Woodrow said.

"It felt great actually cause we were used to the 19 innings so this felt like just a quick game," Woodrow said. "We were just coming at it every inning. We expect to win, we're ready to win and we just never let the pressure in."

O'Dowd was up 2-0 until the bottom of the fifth, when Owen Hamilton hit a two-run single into deep left field. Hamilton is no stranger to heroics, having launched the two-out solo home run that won Drake the MCAL pennant.

Drake head coach Will Mosley said he was expecting this slow start, but wasn't worried.

"Honestly, I expected a hangover, I expected us to be a little sluggish, I expected them to come out of the fire," said Mosley. "I just wanted us to kind of take our time and get back in it. Once we tied it, everybody relaxed, and it was just a matter of time."

O'Dowd head coach Chris Kyriacou was proud of his players, but also had high praise for Drake's consistency in the game.

"Our kids executed, but honestly, Drake just doesn't give you anything," Kyriacou said. "Very rare they make more than one error. In high school baseball that's unique. Hats off to them."

Drake will move on to the second round of the NCS playoffs where they will host against No. 6 Moreau Catholic at 3:30 on Friday.

Senior pitcher Nick Roth is looking forward to Friday after earning the win against O'Dowd.

"I'm feeling really good," Roth said. "Win or lose throughout the next couple games, it's been a hell of a year so hope we're going to finish on a high note."

Hamilton's big postseason continues as Drake moves into semifinals

*By **Ian Ross**, Marin Independent Journal*

POSTED: 05/26/17, 8:04 PM PDT | UPDATED: ON 05/27/2017

Drake's Owen Hamilton has been no stranger to late-inning heroics in this postseason.

With a walk-off home run in the 19th inning of the MCAL championship game already under his belt, Hamilton added a sixth-inning grand slam to his résumé in the North Coast Section Division III quarterfinals against Moreau Catholic on Friday.

Hamilton's blast all but put the game out of reach, increasing Drake's lead to 9-0 at the time. The host Pirates tacked on a 10th run after Jensen Yamane and Gabe Leary were hit by pitches to end the game in the sixth, 10-0 on the mercy rule.

Although Hamilton has made a name for himself this season with his power hitting, that wasn't always the case.

"Last year he batted nearly .400, got like 26 hits but only had one RBI the entire season," Drake coach Will Mosley said. "He was putting pressure on himself. He worked hard in the off- season, playing water polo and in the weight room. He led the MCALs in home runs and he leads our team. Two grand slams in one season and a walk off in the 19th...he's not letting the moment get too big and he's just taking the same swing that he takes in batting practice into games. That's all him. It's his hard work and I'm very proud of the way he's made himself into a great player right now."

The win was the 23rd of the season for the Pirates (23-5), a milestone of sorts for the team.

"In the last 15-20 years, I've seen the records and the best record was 23-6," Mosley said. "Two teams have done it and we have 23 wins right now. I don't know, maybe in the (1950s) or 60s or something (a team won more games), but in current history, no team has had more than 23 wins at Drake."

The third-seeded Pirates will go for win No. 24 and a spot in the NCS final next week on Tuesday or Wednesday against either MCAL foe San Marin or Analy. The No. 10 Mustangs travel to face the No. 2 Tigers — winners of 17 consecutive games — at 1 p.m. on Saturday.

In addition to the wins mark, the Pirates have another milestone in their sights.

"I know there has been… a lot of great teams (at this school) so to tie that record is great, but we want to beat it and be the first team in Drake history to get three banners," starting pitcher Ryan McLaughlin said.

McLaughlin delivered another quality start — the Pirates as a team have yet to give up more than three runs in a game this season — scattering four hits and striking out three over six scoreless innings.

"He's been very consistent this year and today he did a great job," Hamilton said of McLaughlin. "When he gave up a hit, he would bear down and get a groundball just like we needed to turn a double play."

Yamane, the Pirates' shortstop, started double plays in the first and fourth innings to help keep the Mariners (17-9) off the board.

The Pirates began the game with a two-run first inning, getting a triple from Case Delst followed by an RBI single from Nick Roth, a single off the fence from Eamonn Lance, and a second run-scoring single, this one from Eric Woodrow.

The Pirates added a third run in the fifth inning after singles by Roth and Lance. A wild pitch scored Roth to make it 3-0.

The Pirates finally knocked Moreau Catholic starter Alex Pham out of the game in the bottom of the sixth inning.

"We talked about making sure that we come out and attack early because (Pham) throws a lot of fastballs…we executed our game plan perfectly," Mosley said. "We also knew that they didn't have anyone after him so once we got past him…we would be able to pour it on."

The Pirates loaded the bases on a walk, a single and a hit-by-pitch before knocking Pham out of the game with one out and the score still 3-0. Two more walks made it 5-0, then Hamilton went deep to put the game out of reach.

"I think we felt like we had gotten pretty close to getting to (Pham)," McLaughlin said. "He did a good job of keeping the ball down, but he made some mistakes. Owen hit a grand slam again, so we just tried to jump on his mistakes."

Drake advances to baseball section title game

By Marin Independent Journal

POSTED: 05/31/17, 7:49 PM PDT | UPDATED: ON 05/31/2017

All season long, the Drake High baseball team has been eyeing Miramonte. Both teams began the spring 12-0, though the Matadors have yet to lose.

With a 1-0 victory over No. 2 Analy in the North Coast Section Division III semifinals on Wednesday in Sebastopol, the third-seeded Pirates (24-5) set up a date with top-seeded Miramonte (27-0) at noon Saturday in the championship game in Moraga.

"We've been 1 and 2 in the MaxPreps polls pretty much the entire season, so it's fitting we meet up for all the marbles," Drake coach Will Mosley said. "We know them. They're a really, really good team. We're going to have to spend the next two days actually getting better, as funny as that sounds at this point in the season."

To reach the final, the Pirates needed to escape with a road win against an Analy team riding an 18-game winning streak. Senior Nick Roth did what he and fellow starter Ryan McLaughlin have done all season: Dazzle on the mound. Roth allowed four hits over seven innings, striking out 10 batters en route to notching the victory. Case Delst, who doubled to lead off the top of the fourth inning, came around on an Owen Hamilton sacrifice fly for the game's lone run. Isaac Friedenberg, batting eighth in the lineup, went 3 for 3, and Eamonn Lance finished 2 for 2 with a walk.

The Pirates, who won the section title in 2015 when Mosley was an assistant, have given up two runs in three NCS games this spring. They entered Wednesday's contest with a team ERA of 0.54.

"He's been doing it for us all year," Mosley said of Roth. "He pitched with confidence and our team played well behind him. That's our recipe. He did everything we asked of him and more. He went into their place and only allowed one runner to third base. I'm so proud of him and the entire team because they came to play and beat and a really good team.

"I feel really good about what these guys have done up to this point, and I'm confident we're going to compete."

NCS baseball: Drake captures section title with 4-3 win over Miramonte

By **Mark C. Volain**, *Marin Independent Journal*

POSTED: 06/03/17, 5:27 PM PDT | UPDATED: ON 06/04/2017

MORAGA >> Miramonte entered Saturday's North Coast Section Division III championship game looking to cap off what had been a historic season, but Drake wound up as the ones making history.

Not only did Drake end Miramonte's bid at a perfect season, its 4-3 upset victory also earned the Pirates their most victories in a season in school history.

"We expected to win, even knowing that most people expected Miramonte to come out on top," Drake coach Will Mosley said. "What you saw today is what we've been doing all year. Just battle and not let the other team score."

The Pirates (25-5), winners of two NCS titles in the last three years, made it immediately known that they were not intimated by the tall task they were facing, manufacturing a run after Case Delst doubled, a wild pitch moved him to third, and Nick Roth squeeze-bunted him in.

Miramonte (27-1) responded in the bottom of the third by managing to score two runs in an inning where it only recorded one hit. With Casey McGonigle batting, a balk by Drake pitcher Ryan McLaughlin allowed Ben Mollahan to score from third. A few pitches later, McGonigle hit a routine ground ball to first base that was bobbled, allowing McGonigle to reach base and bringing home Jake Hassard to put the Matadors ahead 2-1.

While McLaughlin was not responsible for either run, he picked his team up in the very next inning. Roth walked, Owen Hamilton singled and Eric Woodrow tied the game with a double with two outs. From there, McLaughlin hit a booming two-run double off the left field wall to put the Pirates back ahead 4-2.

The four runs would prove to be enough for McLaughlin, who struck out eight in a complete game, highlighted by an impressive escape job in the sixth.

With no outs and the bases loaded, McLaughlin was able to retire three consecutive batters to limit the damage to one run.

"I've had situations like that before," McLaughlin said. "You really just have to focus on one hitter at a time and trust your defense. It all worked out."

Miramonte managed to get a runner on in the seventh after a one-out single from Nick Foster, but Delst caught him stealing, pretty much ending any chance of a last-stand rally. Delst is said to have described the throw as the best of his life. The final out was made by sophomore second baseman Isaac Freidenberg.

"I felt like maybe we were a little tight, like we were trying too hard," Miramonte coach Vince Dell'Aquila said. "But a 27-0 team is always going to try really hard in a championship game. Sometimes the harder you try, the tougher it gets.

"To be able to get as far as we did was improbable," Dell'Aquila said. "A lot of the guys asked me through the streak if I'd rather lose a game and I said no. It was unfortunate that it happened in the last game, but these players gave it everything they had.

The better team won today."

The Pirates' final two games were against teams on a combined 45-game win streak, a daunting task for any team. But the Pirates have had some magic in them since winning the 19-inning, two-day MCAL championship. Drake needed extra-innings heroics to top Moreau Catholic in the opening round of the NCS tournament and ended Analy and Miramonte's 18 and 27-game respective win streaks by a single run each.

For McLaughlin, Saturday's championship victory finished off what he said has been the most amazing season of his playing career.

"This was the best season I have ever had in my life," McLaughlin said. "I'm never going to forget this team because this whole year was just the most fun I've ever had playing baseball."

Mosley was also unable to recall another season quite like this. "No team in school history has ever done this," Mosley said. "They made their mark and I couldn't be more proud."

The majority of this story was written by Bay Area News Group correspondent Martin Gallegos.

Drake baseball's improbable win ends Miramonte bid for perfection
By Mitch Stephens, Updated 6:25 pm, Monday, June 5, 2017

The script couldn't have been written any better: Miramonte-Orinda's baseball team had a chance to finish undefeated in longtime coach Vince Dell'Aquila's final season.

What's more, the North Coast Section Division 3 title game was played in Miramonte's backyard at St. Mary's College, a perfect venue from which to start a victory parade back to campus.

Unfortunately for the Matadors, no one shared the script with Drake-San Anselmo, an overachieving, underwhelming bunch that second-year coach Will Mosley said "wouldn't pass any initial eye test."

Despite appearances, Drake pulled out a 4-3 victory to end Miramonte's perfect season and claim the school's second NCS title in three years and fourth overall.

The win also took the sting out of a last year's season-ending loss to Miramonte and completed the program's first trifecta of Marin County Athletic League regular-season and playoff titles and the NCS crown.

The Pirates (25-5) also set a school record for victories.

"This team responded to everything we asked of them and every challenge put in front of them," Mosley said.

"Even facing an undefeated team with a lot of motivation, these guys just play with so much heart and play so smart. They made it a season to remember."

It helps to have a team ERA of 0.58 and play virtually flawless defense, led by 5-foot-2, first-team All-MCAL shortstop Jensen Yamane — described by Mosley as "the little engine that could."

With a rotation led by Nick Roth (9-3, 0.82 ERA, 92 strikeouts, 81 innings) and Ryan McLaughlin (9-1, 0.40, MCAL Pitcher of the Year), Drake didn't allow more than three runs in any game this season.

So after Eric Woodrow tied Saturday's game 2-2 in the fourth with an RBI double and McLaughlin followed with a two-run double, Drake had its magic number of four runs.

Miramonte (27-1) responded by loading the bases with no outs in the sixth. But McLaughlin (four-hitter, eight strikeouts) wiggled out of the jam, allowing only a run.

In the seventh, junior catcher Case Delst threw out a would-be base-stealer, all but sealing a terrific game and season for his team.

"I couldn't be prouder of my guys," Dell'Aquila said. "Winning five or 10 games in a row is unique in baseball, let alone 27."

Saturday's win wasn't the only memorable one of the season for the Pirates.

In the section semifinals, Drake broke Analy-Sebastopol's 18-game win streak with a 1-0 victory as Roth struck out 10 and allowed three hits.

On May 20, Drake won the MCAL playoff title 2-1, beating Marin Catholic on a 19th-inning home run by Owen Hamilton in a game that had to be completed the day after it started because of curfew at the park.

"Something magical changed after that," Mosley said. "We had to use our fourth through seventh pitchers. We knew then this season was special. I don't know if it was fate, but that game definitely prepared us for a game like Saturday."

MaxPreps senior writer Mitch Stephens covers high school sports for The Chronicle.

Proclamation

The Town of San Anselmo is pleased to honor the

Sir Francis Drake High School
Varsity Baseball Team
for their historic season and for their amazing MCAL and NCS Championships

Whereas, on Friday, May 19th and Saturday, May 20th, the 2017 Sir Francis Drake High School Varsity Baseball team played Marin Catholic High School for the Marin County Athletic League Championship; and

Whereas, after playing 19 innings over a two-day period, Drake emerged victorious after a walk-off home run in the bottom of the 19th; and

Whereas, on Saturday, June 3rd, Drake entered the final game of the California Interscholastic Federation – North Coast Section championships against Miramonte High School team that was looking for a final victory to cap off a perfect sea- son at 20-0; and

Whereas, through hard work and determination, Drake won the game to become CIF North Coast Section champions; and

Whereas, the team's final two games were played against teams with a combined 45 game win streak; and

Whereas, the team earned the most victories in a single season in the school's history; and

Whereas, the team and coaching staff have brought excitement, pride to the community, and new championship banners to display at the school marking these exceptional accomplishments.

Now, therefore, on behalf of the citizens of San Anselmo, I, Kay Coleman, Mayor of the Town of San Anselmo, do hereby honor Coach Will Mosley, his coaching staff and the entire 2017 Sir Francis Drake Pirates Varsity baseball team for their great achievements.

On this 13th day of June, 2017.
Kay Coleman, Mayor

Marin IJ Baseball Player of the Year: Drake's Nick Roth

POSTED: 06/16/17, 4:53 PM PDT | UPDATED: ON 06/16/2017

Selecting the top player in any sport is always difficult. Electing someone from the 2017 prep baseball season, a Drake High standout in particular, is borderline onerous.

The Pirates had their best season in school history, beginning 12-0 and finishing 25-5 (14-4 MCAL) after winning the league regular-season title, tournament title and the North Coast Section Division III championship. Drake, seeded No. 3 in the section playoffs, upset No. 2 Analy and No. 1 Miramonte — teams on a combined 45-game win streak at the time — in the semifinals and final.

There's Ryan McLaughlin, the MCAL's Pitcher of the Year who also batted .310 and dominated an undefeated Miramonte team in the final game of the spring before wrapping up the season with a 0.45. Then there's postseason hero Owen Hamilton, who in addition to pitching seven scoreless relief innings and belting a walk-off home run in a two-day, 19-inning MCAL title-clinching victory over Marin Catholic, finished the season with a .322 batting average and an ERA of 0.22. Jensen Yamane and Case Delst have been team MVPs at some point during the season, as coach Will Mosley pointed out.

But nobody had quite the season Roth produced. The College of Marin-bound senior recorded a season ERA of 0.78 (the Pirates' was 0.54 combined) with a team-high 92 strikeouts in 81 innings. From the dish, Roth batted a team-high .348 with 14 runs, 17 RBIs and 13 steals.

About the Author

My name is Will Mosley and I am a baseball guy. I am currently a coach, used to be a player, and have always been a fan of the great game of baseball. It has been the only consistent thing in my life and has taken me so many places. I was born in Kansas City, Missouri, and my family moved to Northern California in 1985. I was eight years old and had already played four years of baseball. My parents worked hard, but we moved around a lot and didn't have very much money.

Not sure how it happened, but my dad always managed to get me on teams where, somehow, I was able to do so many incredible things as a youth that most players from low-income families never get a chance to experience. My teammates were often the sons of CEOs, politicians, lawyers, and from many other wealthy families. I traveled from Fairfield, California to Dublin, Ohio on my first baseball trip without my parents at the age of fourteen in 1991. We won the CABA National Tournament that had seventy-two teams, and I was hooked.

The following season, Rob Bruno approached me about joining a team made up of the best players in the Bay Area. Next thing I knew, I was commuting seventy miles from Fairfield to San Jose for baseball practice. Most of the players pulled up in nice cars while my dad and I were rolling in a 1976 Honda Civic hatchback with a weak clutch. Little did I know then, but that team laid the foundation for what is now NorCal Baseball. We were their inaugural team.

Over the past twenty-five years, NorCal baseball has produced two MLB MVPs, ten MLB All-Stars, twenty first-round draft picks, forty-five MLB players, with more than 275 players drafted and over 400 Division I players. I was fortunate enough to be a part of that process. We barely had gas money and I was able to travel the country playing the game that I loved. In 1992, I traveled to Charlotte, North Carolina, where we won the 15 & Under AAU National Championship. I was named the most valuable player. They gave the MVP trophy to the parent that paid for my trip. I thought that was a fair exchange.

At the hotel after the championship game, a coach from another team in the tournament asked if I could play in another World Series tournament in Seattle, Washington the following week. Somehow, we made that happen too. I took a plane up there and returned home on a fifteen-hour bus ride all the way back to Fairfield. I was the only kid riding without an adult on the Greyhound sitting in the back near the bathroom with another championship medal around my neck.

In 1993, I went to Billings, Montana for the American Legion Western Regionals, and then on to Roseburg, Oregon for the World Series with Solano Concrete American Legion as the youngest player on the team. By the time I was sixteen years old, I had already been all over the country and developed a love affair with the game and everything else that comes along with it. I realized that there was value in being a good player. I also became intimately familiar with road trips, hotels, meal money, and girls.

It wasn't until college that I realized how truly rare my baseball experience had been. This may sound weird to some people, but this was the first time I paid attention to my skin color. African-American college baseball players are few and far between. It took some time and a little bit of soul searching, but I found a way to get comfortable and thrive being the only or one of the few African-American players. From high school, to the University of Missouri, Ole Miss, and Sacramento State, there were never more than two of us on the team.

My ability to play baseball gave me the opportunity to travel, get a college degree, and chase my dreams. My experiences as a player have helped shape me into a coach with the ability to connect with players from all backgrounds and skin colors.

In 2004, I traded in my cleats for a fungo bat and a bucket to become a full-time coach. Since then, I have won more games than lost and have taken teams (ages 11-15) to New York, Florida, Colorado, Nevada, Oregon, South Carolina, and Arizona. I have coached more than a dozen MLB draft picks, over fifty baseball scholarship athletes, and hundreds more quality young men. I've taught lessons with a five-year-old in his backyard ballpark and watched him grow into a Division I player twelve years later. I've also had the pleasure of coaching elite teams with rosters filled with the top players in the country for weeks at a time at USA Baseball facilities in Cary, North Carolina for NTIS and in Peoria, Arizona for National Championships.

Although I had already been coaching travel baseball for years, I had never been able to sustain a quality program. I was very comfortable on the field, but a terrible businessman and absent-minded administrator. I spent most of my early coaching career trying to help everyone, and in the end, I only hurt my family and myself. I would regularly have teams of twelve players and only four or five families would pay. I would have to come out of pocket and went home in the hole after every tournament. I never turned a player away because they couldn't pay, and I became a glutton for punishment. Some seasons I didn't have a car and rode to the games with the parents of the players. I would work during the week to pay for my travel expenses and tournament fees on the weekends. It was a labor of love that forced me to do whatever I had to do in order to support my coaching habit and I've had quite a few different jobs:

o   Non-credentialed PE teacher
o   Memberships sales at a fitness club
o   Wrote a newspaper column on fatherhood
o   Life Insurance salesman
o   High School Campus Monitor
o   Sold car stereo equipment
o   Bartender at a nice restaurant
o   Director of Marketing/Admissions at a private school
o   Marketing specialist at a roadwork construction company
o   Owner of an indoor training facility
o   Started a non-profit for lower income student-athletes
o   Field operations director for a technology company
o   Program Site Director for an after-school program
o   Bartender at a comedy club
o   Assistant manager at a retail store
o   Paraprofessional at an elementary school
o   Outreach coordinator at a continuation school
o   UPS Pre Load Manager
o   Education/Work Specialist for a non-profit

My gypsy soul has taken me all over the place and I've learned something at every stop. Getting jobs has never been an issue but finding jobs that allow me to coach was a whole different story. It all made sense based on my youth, during which I attended three elementary schools, two middle schools, and two high schools, one of which I attended twice. I also went to three colleges and played in four different conferences because Mizzou moved from the Big 8 to the Big 12 while I was there.

In 2010, Adam Farb, owner of NorCal Travel Ball (NCTB) and former varsity head coach at Sir Francis Drake High School, paid me out of his own pocket to coach his JV team. I spent five years coaching at the junior varsity level and continued to coach youth teams in the summer and fall.

My youth coaching life took a turn for the better when I met Tucker Sine. He was an influential parent of a twelve-year-old player that was frustrated with the travel baseball programs in Marin, so together, we formed the California Daredevils. Adam and the NCTB staff gave Tucker my name and, after eight months of hard work, we took a group of twelve-year-old players based out of Tiburon, California to Cooperstown, New York and went 10-0 to win the 2014 National Championship.

Tucker provided much-needed stability. He took over all the administrative and financial responsibilities and I could finally just focus on coaching. We started out with one team but have turned into a thriving program that continues to grow each year. That original groups of players and their families, along with Adam and Tucker, are the reasons I have been able to stay in Marin County.

In 2016, I took over as the Varsity baseball coach at Drake HS and became the first African American baseball coach in school history. I inherited a quality program left in great shape by Adam.

The team was coming off an NCS Championship in 2015, and I was looking to continue the winning ways. We underachieved on the field, but a culture of hard work, team play, and determination was born out of the failure.

Appendix

2017 Drake Baseball Staff

Will Mosley – Varsity Head Coach

Kevin Hauschel – Varsity Assistant Coach

Hoss Parnow – Varsity Assistant Coach

Adam Farb – Varsity Pitching Coach/Roving Instructor

Anthony Uyeno – JV Head Coach

Daniel Baptista – JV Assistant Coach

Scott Lance – Freshman Coach

Stephen Henderson – Freshman Coach

2017 Drake Baseball Roster

#1 Jensen Yamane – SS – Senior (c)

#3 Owen Hamilton – 1B/RHP – Senior (c)

#4 Eamonn Lance – LF/C – Sophomore

#5 Isaac Friedenberg – 2B – Sophomore

#6 Bryan McCaffrey – 2B – Senior

#7 Eric Woodrow – OF – Junior

#8 Patrick Brown – 3B – Senior

#9 Ryan McLaughlin – RF/RHP – Junior

#10 Spencer Graves – RHP/1B – Senior

#14 Case Delst – C – Junior (c)

#15 Keegan Pedersen – RHP - Senior (c)

#16 Ryder Morford – OF – Senior

#17 Rocky Clark – DH – Senior

#18 Nick Roth – RHP/3B – Senior (c)

#19 Ian Casey – OF – Junior

#24 Matt Brockley – RF – Senior

#33 Gabe Leary – CF - Junior

We led the nation with a team ERA of 0.54 and only gave up seventeen earned runs in thirty games. We set a school record for wins. We hit four grand slams and two extra inning walk-off home runs in the postseason and received a proclamation from the town mayor.

Even with those eye-popping statistics, what people will remember the most about the 2017 Drake Pirates is the nineteen-inning MCAL championship game versus Marin Catholic that started at 7:00pm on a Friday night and ended on Saturday at 1:30pm.

The greatest game in Marin County Athletic League history didn't just happen overnight, although it felt like it. A whole lot of time, work, and energy went into building a team equipped for the grind. The following section gives a brief description of our culture, our hitting, an interview with our pitching coach Adam Farb, and our program standards.

How We Did It

The 2017 season was a "perfect storm" of sorts. We had a unique combination of experience, youth, intelligence, and a bitter taste in our mouths from the year before. We didn't set out to break the school record in wins or have the lowest ERA in the nation, and we didn't set out to play a nineteen-inning championship game.

In 2016, we lost six games with the lead in the seventh, and we used that as motivation to emphasize the importance of finishing games in 2017. We were able to create a sense of urgency in the way we practiced and played games. We started the season 12-0, and the players began to believe that we could be a very good team.

Our coaching staff focused on creating a sustainable culture with clearly defined roles. We wanted to simplify the game for the players and give them the tools to make the right adjustments. We spent more time on individual skill development than years passed and made a concentrated effort to get significantly better at our weaknesses.

Our Culture

There is so much inherent standing around built into baseball that you better like the guys you are with. Good chemistry is vitally important to a team's success, both on and off the field. With the revolving-door rosters in high school baseball, there is nothing more valuable than a quality culture.

Captains

This year, I had five captains. Most years, I have less. I just wanted to make sure that I had my team's support system in place. I wanted them to share the responsibility and hold each other accountable.

I wanted to know their vision for the season, and work with them to make it happen. I allowed them to create the program standards and encouraged them to take ownership of the team.

There are certain things that a coach can't control but, with a solid group of captains, I can have a better idea about what is really going on with the team. Peer leadership is a powerful tool if used correctly.

I spent a lot of time with my captains away from the field. I cooked for them and we discussed the status of the team on a regular basis throughout the season. They worked together to do the dishes and clean the kitchen as we mapped out a plan together.

If there were problems with teammates, we would discuss a course of action and make it happen. I allowed them to express concerns and we worked together to come up with solutions.
We also watched Warriors games and played PS4 occasionally.

Expectations

Our best players were our hardest workers. It had been that way for years at Drake. The most talented players were also the most relentlessly driven to put in extra work on a daily basis, whether they went 3-3 or 0-3. There were times that I had to lock them out of the field and force them to go home, because too many balls were lost in the dark.

My players set the level of expectations for the team on and off the field. I just told them the truth about what would make them better, and my leaders did the rest. Consistent extra effort was not a requirement, but it had become the norm at Drake, because they had realized that it led to wins.

We had averaged 20 wins per season since 2010 and that provided a level of confidence in everything that they did. They looked at the left field fence where the banners hung and knew that hard work was the only way they got up there.

Off the field, Drake baseball players had a legacy of high academic achievement as well. We won the scholastic award for the highest GPA in NCS Division III the last two years. The players were very aware of what they were a part of and took great pride in being a Pirate.

Competition

In an era where players expect to receive a trophy just for showing up, I spend most of my time teaching my players how to compete. To be able to put up a fight against a tough opponent, they first must learn to compete with themselves. That is why we measure as many things as possible. Steal times, pop times, delivery times, exit speed, bat speed, and anything else we can track with a stopwatch or radar gun. Each day, I challenge my players to be better than they were the day before. The numbers don't lie and become an instant competition. We call it the "Power of the White Board." If we track it and post it, the players automatically care about it a little more once we start counting. Not only do they get better at a necessary skill, but they also learn how to win.

A collection of daily wins usually leads to success. Players don't get better in games. Although they do learn from game experiences, the real improvement always happens in practice or during extra work.

Fun

I enjoy the grind and try to instill that in my players. The roller coaster ride of a season is fun to me, and I truly try to get them to live in each moment. We joke around, laugh when something funny happens, and still manage to work very hard most of the time.

That looseness allows the players to relax on game day because they enjoy being on the field with their teammates. Our players don't have to put on a serious game face to compete. We usually don't play well when we aren't having fun, but I guess that goes for everyone.

Baseball is a game and should be played accordingly.

Our Hitting

Hitting a baseball is the most imperfect act in all the ball sports. To get a hit, batters must succeed on two levels. The first task is making solid contact with a ball only nine inches in circumference with a 2 5/8 round bat barrel. The second task is not hitting the ball to the other team while being outnumbered nine to one.

Mechanics & Drills

The only thing that a hitter can do to swing the odds of success back into his favor is to hit the ball harder and farther. There is nothing like the joy that comes when you hit a baseball just right. It feels like the ball is weightless as it hits the bat and explodes into the sky. Trotting around the bases after a homerun is an awesome feeling.

We use the measurement of ball exit speed mph to provide accurate and immediate feedback. Exit speed mph has a direct correlation to ball flight and distance. For hitters to consistently post high mph numbers, they must learn how to generate power, be on time, and maintain balance on a consistent basis.

We always work with failure in mind and, therefore, focus on progress not perfection. Every low mph or "bad swing" that a hitter takes exposes a flaw in his mechanics. The 4-S foundation section breaks down each part of the swing and provides a blueprint for hitters to refer to when there is a mechanical breakdown.

Here are the most common reasons for low mph exit speeds:
o   Pulling head/stepping in the bucket

o   Dropping hands

o   No or late hip drive/turn

o   Front arm lockout/rolling over
o   Off balance

o   Weight moving forward/out in front

o   Dropping back shoulder

o   Not finishing swing

4-S Foundation

1-Stance
2-Step
3-Swing
4-Statue

Points of Emphasis
o   Balance throughout swing
o   Limited head movement
o   Top hand fist toward the pitcher at contact
o   Back knee to the ball
o   Front knee slightly bent at contact
o   Hips start before hands

o   Finish high

Hitting Drills

No Ball Drills
o   Bat behind the back
o   Slaps

Whiffle Ball Drills
o   Top hand swings with training paddle (side toss or front toss)
o   Bottom hand swings with training paddle (side toss or front toss)
o   Back behind the back (tee, side toss or front toss)

Tee Drills
o   Regular swings
o   Crow hops (two steps)
o   Bounce around (start behind and bounce to swing side)
o   Back leg kick up
o   Front leg backward lift
o   Front to back hop

Med Ball Drills
o   Sit-up throw
o   Standing strong side throw
o   Standing weak side throw
o   Sit-up strong side throw
o   Sit-up weak side throw

Approach

Our goal as an offense is to dominate the outer half of the plate. We have a short porch to left field at our place, and we want to dare pitchers to throw our right-handed hitters inside. The only place to get extra base hits is the right centerfield gap on our rectangular-shaped field. We are always talking hitting and emphasize being on time to the fastball away.

One through nine in the order needs to be able to do damage. We want to apply pressure to the pitcher by being tough outs. Our hitters are taught to recognize breaking balls and study what to expect in plus and minus counts.

We take pride in hitting foul balls with two strikes because we understand that each swing gets us closer to being on time to the next one. The players have learned that the best way to time a strike is to swing at it. The only pitches we want to take are the balls out of the zone.

We hunt fastballs away early in the count, looking for that "get me over" strike. We want to make the pitcher uncomfortable early and often. We teach our players to take aggressive hacks with bad intentions in plus counts and to take a wider stance with two strikes and battle to stay alive.

In 2017, we had eight players with at least sixteen hits and our hero changed from game to game. I truly believe you win with the bottom of your lineup. Most teams have good hitters in the first five spots, but the great teams do damage 7-9 and set the table for the top.

We approach every game trying to zap the energy from the opposing pitcher like a "boss battle" in an old-school video game. Each foul ball, ground ball, pop-up, line drive, or good take gets us closer to the bullpen. With high school, pitch counts and rest rules; it is a win to get deep into the opposing team's pitching staff.

Of course, we would love ten hits a game, but we are just looking for three good at-bats with runners in scoring position and two outs. We believe that two-out hits are golden, and RBIs are platinum. To score runs against a team with good defense, you must come through in the clutch.

We won eight one-run games. We also hit four grand slams and two walk-off homeruns in extra innings. In the NCS Championship game, we got two singles, two doubles, and three RBIs, all with two outs, in the 4th inning. I truly believe that consistency in our approach allowed us to be successful when it mattered most.

Our Pitching

Interview with Pitching Coach Adam Farb

Q: Drake has had some pretty impressive pitching staffs, how did this one stack up?
A: Wow, I think you'd have to say that as a staff, they were the best of a great bunch. 39 runs in 30 games! You have the numbers there - may I peek? (reads the stats). Team ERA of 0.54, all 5 pitchers under 1.00 ERA, and then the craziest one: 216 strikeouts to 48 walks! We had a run of 4 pitchers who all were drafted, but the results this team had… yeah, I think they rank #1.

Q: Well, let's get right to it then… How'd you do it?
A: There's no simple answer but for me, but the foundation of the whole thing is culture. Culture over everything.

Q: So how does that play out? Can you be specific?
A: If you walk into this program as a Freshman pitcher, daily, you are working next to guys who at one point were JUST LIKE YOU and are now among the elite pitchers in their region. You have role models to fashion your own positive idea of what you can be as a pitcher and a clear idea of what it takes to get there. So that's #1.

And just as important, competitiveness is a core value. We compete in unique and constant ways. That pays huge dividends in big moments.

Q: Let's get into that second part. What do you do to foster competitiveness in your pitchers?
A: We need a pitcher to compete for his team; we need him to be willing to take the team and put it on his

back when needed. So we try get creative when it comes to competition. For example, one thing that has been great over time is that we create challenges where the entire team gets a reward or consequence, depending on whether the pitcher succeeds.

So let's say: Complete an inning giving up no runs while throwing a maximum of two fastballs; or the whole staff must throw 70% breaking ball strikes in a complete game.

In 2011, we created an in-season, in-game challenge for our immature Sophomore pitcher who was our #2 guy and the critical component if we were going to win a title. It was a series of challenges that he had to get 100% success rate on and the entire team won a steak dinner if he succeeded. In the final game of his three-week challenge, it came down to this one: "Start every inning with a breaking ball and throw them for above 50% strikes." Through six innings, he had thrown three of the six for strikes. So we let him go out for the 7th. It came down to one pitch...

He threw it for a strike and the entire team went nuts. Do you think the pressure of HAVING TO DELIVER for his teammates had anything to do with his outstanding performance in our league playoff game when he beat our rival school to get us into the Championship Game? I sure as heck do.

Q: So how did that culture shape this year's staff?
A: They'd been with me since they started HS - so the continuity and familiarity helped. Four of them got to train alongside Joe Ryan, who was dominant, up to 95 mph, drafted by the Giants, etc. ... They got to see and play on the 2015 team that didn't throw a pitch over 83 mph all season and yet was an elite staff. They got to see Will Martel - a lefty who threw in the high seventies- turn into "THE MAN" and lead his team to a section title. They were part of the daily preparation over four years that allowed them to hopefully be the best version of themselves.

Take the top two arms on the team as examples: Nick Roth was the ace of the staff. He had thrown six innings the night before in a dominant thirteen-strikeout performance to get the team into the Championship. Nick is like 5'9". He's thick and strong as a bull. For him, it was all about flexibility and arm care - most of our work last season was just to prepare him to be healthy and strong. By his senior year, he already knew who he was as a pitcher. It was all about fine-tuning.

Ryan McLaughlin was a totally different deal. We did more mechanical work together than maybe any pitcher I've ever worked with. Ryan is 6'3", deadlifts over 400 pounds, and can jump out of the gym. He's an incredible athlete in some ways. But he's stiff as hell. He's an incredibly accurate thrower and he releases the ball closer to home plate than most big leaguers. So he was throwing like 78-81 mph, but the ball got on hitters quick. For him, most of the in-season work was on pitch development: his changeup has always been a plus pitch, so we made him use his breaking ball more often.

Each guy brought their own strengths to the staff. Each guy had different things they were working to improve. The culture of pitching development that was in place allowed them to be themselves. They adopted the work ethic and philosophy on pitching that we've always had and made it their own. They built on that foundation.

Q: You mentioned a philosophy on pitching. What is your philosophy?
A: It starts with the individual. No two kids are the same, so we are very individual in our approach to building pitchers. But within that, I think there are three fundamental tenets in what we do: (1) Elite Physical Preparation; (2) Pound the Freakin' Zone; and (3) Pitch Shaping.

Q: What does Elite Physical Preparation entail?

A: First, we do physical assessments of pitchers (such a Functional Movement Screen) so we know where our pitchers need more attention. Every pitcher has different physical needs and they need to be trained with an individual focus. That information has helped us get more specific in our mobility or lifting programs.

Second, we are religious about arm care and recovery. We use the TAP and Driveline plyo balls on sub-maximal throws; our pitchers use elite recovery tools like the Arm-Aid arm mas- sager, Electro-Stim as well as surgical tubing. Players throw through soreness, but we don't mess around with PAIN or serious injury.

Third, we manage the calendar and training cycle so pitchers can peak physically in the middle to end of the season. To do that, we shut our pitchers down for the fall and begin their ramp-up and training in November. After the ramp-up, we go through a 4-6-week pure velocity training phase. Each pitcher will have a different pace to their off-season based on fitness level, arm health, and mentality. But in the velocity phase, we want them competing their tails off. A lot of progressive modern training programs emphasize pulldowns or running throws. We didn't really have room or appropriate flooring to do pulldowns in our indoor space, and we have had similar gains of 5-6 mph per player on average without utilizing running throws. We ran a whole velocity training program in our old locker room - sometimes you must use what you got!

And finally, is our throwing program. Typically, our pitchers throw six days a week and five of those days involve pitch execution.

So, let's say we have a starter who will pitch once a week - his weekly program would look something like:

Day 1- Pitch in Game
Day 2- Catch Play & Core Work Day (long toss as far as it feels good to throw)
Day 3- Flat Ground Day 4 - Bullpen Day 5 - OFF DAY
Day 6- Bullpen
Day 7- Flat Ground

Not every pitcher follows the same routine. Some guys prefer throwing two bullpens a week, others like just one pen. Some guys like to throw 10-15 pitches off a mound the day before they pitch. We don't dictate their routine, but we do dictate that they throw six days a week while healthy and that five of those days involve pitch execution.

Q: Okay, so what do you mean by Pound the Freakin' Zone?

A: Every team wants their pitchers to throw strikes. We are more specific. Strike percentages on each pitch type are charted and worked on. We strive for 65% strikes with every pitch in a pitcher's arsenal. Less than that, and we consider that pitch not ready. We strive for 70% strikes with each pitch, but that's a tough goal. Over 65% with the Fastball and at least one off-speed pitch is critical to a pitcher's success within our system.

If a pitcher is below this threshold, that spans additional command work, and we work together with the player to solve this problem. I think some coaches feel like they must choose between encouraging and being demanding. But to me, having a growth mindset and demanding results do not have to be opposites.

Q: Alright, that covers the first two - what's the last one - Pitch Shaping - mean?

A: What makes a pitch "good"? All great pitches are not alike! So we start with having players understand their desired pitch shape. Oh, you are learning a change-up? Well, does it move from glove side to arm side? Does it also have some drop to it? If not, it doesn't have the required pitch shape.

Pitch Shaping provides great external cues for the pitcher and gives a chance to evaluate what the ball is doing more so than a pitcher's "mechanics," which I think are over-coached and generally poorly coached. We want players' minds externally focused - (How can I make the ball do this?) rather than internally focused (What does my glove-side arm do?).

Internal focus DOES NOT WORK very often in sports. Everyone knows if you want to slow down a hitter on a hot streak, ask them to describe how their hands work. It shifts their focus, activates the wrong part of their brain, and they will not be the same. So, as a pitching coach, my role is to guide the player to be their best self. Allowing them to visualize the shape of their pitch flight unlocks the creative side of their brain and frees them up to make the changes the game is dictating that they need to make. I don't necessarily understand all the cognitive science behind this, but I do know this stuff really works!

Q: So do you think the culture and the way the guys trained explains the way the season went?

A: Honestly, I don't think so. The season these kids had defies rational explanation. Dark Magic was somehow at work here. Literally everything that could have gone right went right for us.

Sure, we did a lot right. We couldn't have asked for a better work ethic and focus from the staff! But we had Ryan McLaughlin throwing 78-81 mph go for a 0.32 ERA in almost 90 innings on the mound. We had Owen Hamilton, a 72-mph submariner who was good for 1-2 outs at a time go SEVEN SHUT-OUT INNINGS in our defining game! We had Keegan Pedersen, who required multiple surgeries on his landing leg from an old football injury, who was phenomenally effective in short outings (the kid was in so much pain from his ankle injury that he couldn't throw for long. And he wanted to keep pitching. His doctor gave the okay. So he kept throwing, but we reduced his bullpens and flat grounds to twelve pitches maximum. Adapt or die!).

So, no, I don't think our culture or training is directly responsible for the result. But I know that the magic of that season was fueled by the work and passion that our guys put into it. The tools, techniques, and strategies we used don't explain the season, but it sure INCREASED OUR ODDS of success.

Q: So what was special about the pitchers on this team?

A: A couple months before the season, Owen Hamilton was returning to throwing after not pitching his entire junior year with some nagging shoulder injuries. It wasn't going well. He was trying to throw more "over the top" for some reason and that was putting his shoulder into extension early. Well, not to get too lost in it, but it was slow and straight and looked un- comfortable. Keegan asks me, "Hey, coach, what do you think of Owen dropping down and throwing submarine?" He had a whole case laid out to make, but I was on-board immediately! We presented it to Owen, showed him some basics, and gave him the choice.

I tell that story because it's the clearest example of something that I think was true of this team: they chose their own path to excellence. My role was just to help them get there.

Q: OK, let's get into the nineteen-inning game. What do you remember?
A: First, I was nervous. Not for the kids. For me. I mean, this was only my second game back in the dugout - I hadn't called a game for Ryan since he was a Freshman. I didn't want to screw it up for them!

In the early part of the game, Ryan was good enough, but I don't think he was super-sharp, you know? It wasn't until the 4th or 5th inning that he had all three pitches going, and he was less effective throwing fastballs inside than normal. His inside fastball sets up all his out pitches, so not having that going was a big concern and I think we even had him throw a little on the side between innings to dial it in. In the 5th, he walked the nine batter with one out, but I'd say after that moment, something clicked and he was dominant from then on. They had no real chance to score his last 4 ½ innings. You must remember that Ryan had been the #2 pitcher all year: he put up incredible stats, but he didn't throw much against the best teams we faced. This was a big moment for him! So, in every way, it was really a tremendous outing. One run in nine innings. Ninety-nine pitches, I think, in nine innings. Sixty-six percent strikes. Did it with all three pitches. Competed his tail off. Awesome performance.

But then the game really gets interesting in the 10th. We decide to go to Keegan, mostly I think because Will trusted Keegan to not let the moment get to him. And sure enough, Keegan comes out throwing strikes but gives up a couple hits, and with two outs, Pedersen, their two-hitter, hits a flare that looks like it's going to fall just over our second baseman's head, but he makes a great leaping, falling catch and we go on. Keegan, who can barely walk, is hopping out to congratulate him. He had to get help to get to the bench and went straight to our trainer!

And then the bottom of the 10th, it looks like we're about to win, right? And thank goodness because our pitcher is lying on his back with one shoe on and the other foot is being worked on and re-taped by the trainer! So it's bases loaded, one out, our cleanup hitter up. We're all mentally preparing for the celebration a little bit. And somehow, we fly out into a 9-2 double play and Keeg has to go back out to the mound. But he can barely walk, his ankle hurt so much, and they are coming to the heart of their order. And the kid throws like an eleven-pitch inning and mows them down, 1-2-3. Incredible! I remember being aware that the game had become special. But in the moment, I'm not thinking about that much - I'm thinking, "What the hell are we gonna do if we don't score?"

And so we go to the 11th with Owen all warmed up, but Keegan still on the mound, limping badly just to get out there and probably the adrenaline starting to fade a little. And he walks the leadoff guy - he just can't go any further. So now we have to go to Owen. Who pitches us out of the 11th and even strikes out three hitters. But to me, the stuff didn't look great and I think I said something like "We need to score soon; he can't hold them for long."

And even though they get their leadoff man aboard, I think in like five of his six other innings, they can't get the big hit and he DOES hold them off, all the way to seven shutout innings. His changeup - a "work in progress" since December - suddenly turns into a weapon against lefties in those innings. Tired hitters get fooled by the pitch over and over again and Owen is able to continue to do his job all the way up past midnight. And the defense… man oh man… From the 3rd to the 19th inning, seventeen innings without an error. On a choppy field. In dim lighting. And not only was the defense mistake-free, but they turn a few double plays, and make a couple of exceptional plays. Case makes two huge blocks in the 18th inning - either of those gets away and they score. Stuff like that. It was a remarkable team performance.

Q: So the game is suspended after eighteen innings, tied 1-1. How'd you sleep?

A: Not well. I got home at like 12:45 am, and I had to wake up at 6 for work. I couldn't be there for the 19th inning. I think I was up until about 3 am. Wrote up the scouting report and pitch plan for Spencer Graves (Spencer was going to come in and pitch in the 19th). I knew that would get to Case and he would call a good game for Spencer. But it sucked a lot to not be there to see it through.

Q: Were you comfortable going to Spencer Graves in that spot?

A: No. I don't think I was comfortable from the 9th inning on! Spencer had thrown pretty well all year, but he was fighting an uphill battle to get innings on that staff, and I think he had mentally packed it in a little bit in the few weeks before that game. But he throws a decent breaking ball, and more important - he's a competitor!

   Right before the seniors started HS, I was able to coach them in a travel ball tournament. Spencer ended up throwing a complete game and winning the championship game of that tournament. However he was feeling about his role this season, he never stopped being that kind of winner.

Q: Isn't there more to a win than just the pitcher?

A: Of course, but that's not what I mean by being a winner. It's not about the result of the game. It's about winning a pitch or winning an at-bat. It's the ability to be at your best when the adversity is highest.

   I believe WINNING is a skill that can be trained over time. Some kids come to us further along on that than others. Nick Roth had good skills, but no idea how to finish at-bats or battle through tough times early in his HS career. Ryan McLaughlin had to learn how to use different pitches to win at-bats. But Spencer…he competes angry. Always has. We never had to train that skill with him - we just had to remind him who he is!

   Each individual guy learned how to win with the tools they had. They had done the big work to get ready, and as the season went on, they did the fine-tuning work to be able to win at-bats against good hitters. The story of this pitching staff to me is inspirational: ordinary kids can do extraordinary things if they care enough and put in the work they need.

Drake High School Baseball Program Standards

Practice Expectations:

Build confidence through quality repetition
- Be prepared to call people out and to be called out
- Hold each other accountable to team standards
- Be able to work on accomplishing your goals with no one watching
- Maximize reps

Game Mentality:

Control your breathing and enjoy the challenge
- Failure is never fatal, and success is never permanent, and be aware of yourself and the game you're playing
- Play every game the same way

Offensive Approach:

Hunt speeds and drive the ball gap-to-gap
- Every pitch gets you closer to being on time for the next one
- Make the pitcher sweat

Defensive Skill Sets:

Play the game in between pitches
- 9 on 1
- Have a conversation with each other throughout the game
- Don't let errors snowball
- Maintain energy throughout a baseball game

Pitching Style:

Attack hitters with purpose down in the zone
- Compete regardless of circumstance
- Work ahead in the count
- Don't waste pitches

Baserunning:

- *Cause problems for the other team and not us*
- Have field awareness, and check infielder/outfielder position
- Know your matchups (Steal time, Pitcher/Catcher times, etc.)
- Make your mistakes at 100%

Miscellaneous:

- Love your teammates and enjoy playing with them
- Everyone has a job to do

92931339R00055

Made in the USA
San Bernardino, CA
07 November 2018